Urban Planning for
Social Welfare

PRAEGER SPECIAL STUDIES IN
U.S. ECONOMIC AND SOCIAL DEVELOPMENT

Urban Planning for Social Welfare

A MODEL CITIES APPROACH

Edward M. Kaitz
Herbert Harvey Hyman

PRAEGER PUBLISHERS
New York • Washington • London

The purpose of Praeger Special Studies is to make specialized research in U.S. and international economics and politics available to the academic, business, and government communities. For further information, write to the Special Projects Division, Praeger Publishers, Inc., 111 Fourth Avenue, New York, N.Y. 10003.

PRAEGER PUBLISHERS
111 Fourth Avenue, New York, N.Y. 10003, U.S.A.
5, Cromwell Place, London S.W.7, England

Published in the United States of America in 1970
by Praeger Publishers, Inc.

Library of Congress Catalog Card Number: 69-19333

Printed in the United States of America

PREFACE

"The cities are dying!" This is a cry that has been sounded all too frequently in recent years. Numerous symptoms are noted by those making this assertion: the flight of the middle class; the growth of the slum areas; and the deterioration in public services provided for the remaining citizens. In spite of the federal and state governments' rapidly increasing investment in welfare, health, education, job training, housing, and a whole range of other programs, the urban crisis continues to grow. Many have stated that the slum cannot be rehabilitated, that the solution lies in building new towns. Yet, even if this solution were practical, there are millions of persons who would be residing in the slums for years to come. These deprived citizens have been awakened to the new opportunities that await them. Their expectations of breaking out of their cycle of poverty have been heightened. Yet, the progress of public and private efforts has been too limited to make much of an impact on the masses of the poor. The masses, seeing some of their people making it, feel cheated. They feel that the government has not been serious about helping most of them. They cry out at the "tokenism" of the assistance offered.

With their hopes aroused out of proportion to the actual resources available, many have turned to an angry militancy. Feeling deceived by the limited resources of the numerous federal programs recently enacted to help them, many have rebelled against involving themselves in any kind of public program. And, at the same time, they have been quick to react to any felt offense to their pride. Riots, looting, setting of fires, and direct confrontations with authority symbols, especially the police, educators, and welfare officials, have resulted. Private and public officials closely concerned with rehabilitating the slums have observed this situation with despair. They witness the slums growing more deteriorated and volatile in spite of the increased resources made available to those in the poverty areas.

Yet, there are those who see hope. They tend to look, not just at the poverty areas, but at the whole metropolitan region, of which the poverty areas represent a small proportion. From this wider perspective, they see vitality, growth, burgeoning affluence, new schools, roads, and shopping centers. From their perspective, the slum areas, while growing, are growing far less rapidly than the affluence of the suburbs. The cities are no longer viewed as independent entities with a life of their own. Rather, they are seen as part of a larger metropolitan whole, in which the city and its suburbs are interrelated. Unfortunately for those with this wider perspective, the city and its surrounding towns are politically autonomous, with very different constituencies. And the needs of these constituencies are quite different. Because the political fact of a city's autonomy is inconsistent with the planner's socioeconomic view of a city as part of a metropolis it becomes all the more necessary to give attention to the cities and the urban crisis and to treat the city as the independent entity it really is. It is for this reason that the cities and their problems will be examined apart from their relationship to the metropolis.

Even while there are apostles of despair, there are also apostles of hope, who believe that something can be done to pump new life into the cities, and especially to improve conditions in the slums. In a major issue (November 20, 1967) devoted to this question, Newsweek gave its program for hope. It based its "Time for Advocacy" editorial on three premises:

> The first is that America has so far failed
> to deliver to many citizens, and particularly
> to many Negroes, that measure of equality
> that lies at the heart of the American idea.

A second premise is that America has
the ability to make that delivery: surely
the most prosperous and powerful nation in
history, which concerns itself with poverty,
discrimination and deprivation around the
world, can successfully apply its vast resources to these widespread ills at home.

A third premise is more arguable: that
America has, or can generate, the WILL to
solve its racial problems. (p. 32)

Another major magazine, _Fortune_, devoted an entire
issue (January, 1968) to the role business can play
in the urban crisis. Its editorial stated:

It is now about four months since the great
urban race riots of 1967 ended. It is,
quite a few people believe, about five months
until the riots of 1968 begin.

It is a major theme of this issue of
FORTUNE that the crisis in race relations
is of manageable proportions.

If we really are looking to business to
provide some leadership in the cities, what
may be needed most of all is a change that
will require no new laws, but simply some
new attitudes . . . an . . . intense feeling
of involvement with the city on the part of
the businessmen. (excerpts, pp. 127, 128)

This hope is echoed in government circles and is
manifested by the passage of the most comprehensive
piece of urban legislation since the enactment of the
Social Security Act in the 1930's. This is the
Demonstration Cities and Metropolitan Development
Act of 1966, better known as the Model Cities program. And there is also the hope voiced in the private sector. Major foundations have increased their
funding of anti-poverty programs. Numerous national
and civic groups have created special urban funds to
support governmental efforts. And thousands of

individuals, many from the affluent suburbs, have
offered their direct assistance to the poor. Finally, "The Poor People's March" in May, 1968, represented a demonstration, by the poor themselves, of
their newfound energy to plead their case directly
to the Congressional lawmakers in support of those
programs, such as Model Cities, housing, and economic development, needed to assist them "Upward Bound."
Thus, amidst the poverty, crime, disease, lack of
adequate housing, and poor education, are heard new
voices trying to translate this attitude of hope into
deeds to wipe out despair and poverty.

Regardless of one's perspective or attitude, a
major crisis does exist in our poverty areas. The
object of Chapter 1 is to examine some of the causes
of poverty, which are seen as multiple in nature and
national in scope. They tend to be so interrelated
that they feed on each other and thereby compound the
problem. These causes are also usually the direct
outgrowth and the unanticipated consequence of positive values held by a majority of citizens. These
values, when expressed in the form of programs to
meet the majority's needs, tend to favor those needs
over those of our more disadvantaged citizens. In
turn, the less favored are inadvertently hurt by their
failure to participate in or by their exclusion from
these programs. Although the residents of the urban
slums suffer the most, a number of those in suburban
and rural areas are also adversely affected. The
reader should therefore bear in mind that while primary attention in this study will be given to the
crisis of our urban communities, the problems described as prevalent in our cities are also present
in varying degrees in the rest of the nation.

Chapter 1 will focus on some of the causes that
have had their effect on the cities, and then on:

   (1) The Quantative and Qualitative Aspects
       of Urban Poverty;

   (2) Legislative Attempts to Cope with Poverty;
       and

(3) The Model Cities Program's Attack on
    Poverty.

The following chapters will be devoted to an
analysis of the Model Cities program as a governmental effort to bring the national will to bear upon
the problems of the cities. Special emphasis will
be devoted to the role of planners and Model Cities
residents as potential citizen planners in rebuilding
the slums, to the problems inherent in attempting to
build the "partnership" of citizen and city official,
and to the potential conflicts that can be and already have been engendered by the coordination required in the program. The authors' experience with
New York City's Model Cities program will be cited
in our discussion of these issues.

The two authors were involved in the initial
planning of the program's human resource components,
one as a Model Cities planner and the other as a
consultant to New York City's Human Resources Administration. At the time of their involvement in the
Model Cities program, there were no Housing and Urban
Development Department (HUD) guidelines specifying
the nature of the planning process expected from the
cities applying for Model Cities grants. Through
extensive counseling within the Human Resources Administration (HRA), and with other city agencies, the
authors were able to develop planning concepts that
(1) encompassed the comprehensiveness HUD sought to
achieve in the planning process; (2) permitted the
flexibility needed to effect community involvement in
that planning; and (3) developed a beginning rationale for selecting priorities from among competing demands for human services. These concepts evolved
through a trial-and-error process over a period of
more than nine months. Many of these concepts were
happy accidents.

Consequently, when the first four HUD planning
guidelines were issued, there was a happy coincidence
between what HUD's planning criteria required and the
authors' framework for planning and delivering human
services. Unfortunately, a change of administration at

HRA resulted in a change of direction in that agency's involvement in the Model Cities programs. While the concepts the authors developed became less relevant for Model Cities planning with HRA, these concepts continued to be highly relevant in the community where the planning actually occurred.

As a consultant to one of the three Model Cities areas in New York City, one of the authors later sought to effect the use of such a planning framework. He was only partially successful, because of the reality factors cited in Chapter 4 on citizen participation. The chief impediment to this more comprehensive approach was the prior influence on many of the citizen planners of the anti-poverty program. Only since the completion of this New York City's area Model Cities plan have many of these citizens become aware of the similarities between the Model Cities and the anti-poverty project planning. Many groups have subsequently asked for specific assistance in designing a comprehensive plan for the second year of the Model Cities program. These groups became aware of many of the shortcomings of their plan and saw the relevance of this book's comprehensive approach to the planning process. Some of them have already used the book.

The authors' experiences in the HRA and as consultants to the Model Cities program have reinforced their belief in the relevance of HUD's comprehensive approach to planning. The authors are also aware of the need of professional planners, city administrators, and citizen planners to understand the implications of this comprehensive approach before they attempt to implement such a planning process.

The objective of this book then is not only to describe the difficulties in such planning, but also to provide a practical framework for such planning. The authors are convinced that the planning framework they developed is relevant in any type of comprehensive planning even though the concepts are the outgrowth of a Model Cities planning process. Furthermore, the authors also believe that the planning

process outlined in this book is feasible in cities
as large and complex as New York City and as small
as Winooski, Vermont, the smallest of the Model Cities
communities. It is only the scale on which these
services must be delivered that is vastly different.

CONTENTS

LIST OF TABLES

Urban Planning for
Social Welfare

CHAPTER **1** THE NATURE OF
URBAN POVERTY

CAUSES OF POVERTY

Powerlessness of Cities

In a brilliant summation of "The Great Change"
that has taken place in our urban communities, Professor Roland Warren identified at least seven such
changes in his book, The Community in America. His
basic thesis is that "the 'great change' in community
living includes the increasing orientation of local
community units toward extra-community systems of
which they are a part, with a corresponding decline
in community cohesion and autonomy." What this statement means is that in every aspect of living, decisions are made outside the community which affect
every resident living within it. And they have little
control over how and why these decisions are made.
For example, the American Medical Association's stand
in opposition to our current Medicare program for the
elderly held up enactment of this vital program for
years. The elderly in the local communities either
went without care or were forced to depend on the
goodwill of their family physicians or the inadequate
resources of the municipal hospitals. In another instance, the Federal Housing Authority's (FHA) long-
standing practice against insuring loans for new
construction or rehabilitation of housing located in

The authors wish to acknowledge the assistance
of Alan Kohler in collecting information for this
chapter, particularly the historical data dealing
with legislation.

the poverty areas was one of the key factors that led
to their rapid deterioration, while city officials,
lacking their own financial resources, were helpless
to offset this practice. Decisions about laws,
styles, and professional practices are made outside
the community in both private and public circles and
these decisions affect those in the local communities.
What this means is that officials and residents in
urban communities are losing control of their cities
to outside forces, including state and federal governments, national corporations, and national social,
economic, and cultural institutions.

In light of this trend, the cities are relatively
powerless to make decisions that affect the quality
of life of the city as a whole. How much more powerless are the poverty sub-communities within the cities
to obtain changes they consider important. For example, minority groups have been pressing hard to gain
greater control over the educational system in New
York City. But, to accomplish such a major change requires a change in the state statutes. This "decentralization" of educational authority had the blessing
of the Mayor and other important civic groups. Yet,
the controversy that surrounded the issue resulted in
only a "watered-down" promise of the change desired
by the leaders in the poverty areas. Whereas the May-
or was responsive to the poverty areas, the State Legislature was not, in turn, responsive to the Mayor.
As in this illustration, practically all federal programs, whether anti-poverty, community mental health,
manpower, or housing, are governed by guidelines and
regulations that drastically limit the city's capacity
to determine their use. Thus, the extra-community
locus of power represents an important limiting causal
factor that prevents the city officials from changing
the conditions of the poverty areas within their political jurisdiction.

Population Mobility

Another cause of the urban problem is related to
the mass shifts of population within America. About
30 per cent of the families in the United States move
every year. The more affluent and stable families

within the cities have been steadily migrating to the
suburbs. In turn, their places have been increasingly taken by the migration of rural Southeran families
and Puerto Ricans. This mass migration has upset the
economic and social equilibrium of the cities; it has
steadily undermined the previously existing stabilizing social forces within the city. As those from the
poverty areas move up the economic ladder, they
move into better parts of the city. These movements
upset the political, economic, social, and cultural
life of the city that characterized the former occu-
pants who settled there. Enclaves of ethnic groups
living together are broken up and replaced by other
groups which have as yet had too little time to form
their own cultural and social systems consistent with
their values. This mass migration has had a number
of consequences, which have themselves become causes
affecting the health of the cities, and which have
tended to reinforce the conditions of poverty.

Loss of Economic Viability

First, the economic viability of the city has become reduced as the more affluent families migrate
and their social and cultural institutions move out
with them to the suburbs. This has lowered the capacity of the city government to render the services
needed in increasing measure by the poorer citizens
who replace them. In turn, it has forced the cities
to turn to higher forms of government to gain financial resources just to maintain a barely adequate
level of services. In doing this, the capacity of
the local government to make decisions about what
services will be provided and how they will be rendered has been greatly reduced. This chain of actions
has created urban instability and increased frustration on the part of the poor, whose expectations are
never quite realized because they are at the mercy of
decisions over which they and the city fathers may
have little control. This has been especially evident
in the anti-poverty and Model Cities programs where
control and influence are diminishing, in spite of
the fact that these programs are supposed to have a
profound and direct influence on the lives of the
poor.

Breakdown in Personal Relationships

Second, the swift changes wrought by mass population movements have tended to break down the informal,
personal relationships that had been in existence for
some time. Services that were formerly performed by
families and neighbors are now performed by bureaucratic organizations: the public welfare department;
a homemaker service; or a public health system. Not
only do the poor have less control over the services
that were once performed by informal, personal arrangements, but their relationships to their neighbors
have also become more impersonal as people have moved
in and out of apartments and neighborhoods at a rapid
pace. Not only do the poor have fewer services to assist them, but these are performed by impersonal bureaucratic organizations that view the poor as numbers
or cases rather than people. There is less responsiveness on the part of a depersonalized community to
offer help to those in need, whether through direct
contact in the form of volunteer personal services or
through willingness of the more affluent to pay higher
taxes to hire civil servants to perform these services
in their behalf. Thus, the mass migration into and
out of the central cities has created factors that
have made the average American less knowledgeable
about, and responsive to, the needs of the poor. And
the bureaucratic institutions created to serve the
poor are too impersonal and rigid to meet the individual needs of the poor as people.

Economic Inequality

Another cause of the conditions of the cities
stems from the economic inequalities between their
needs and the resources to pay for them. Among the
three levels of government, the city has traditionally had the narrowest tax base. Not only has the tax
base been further reduced by the movement of the more
affluent residents and commercial firms from the city,
but their primary source of income, the property tax,
has reached the point of saturation. Any increase in
that tax results in a more rapid out-migration of
those property owners in the best position to pay such
a tax. Sales, income, corporate, and excise taxes as

major sources of revenue have already been preempted
by the state and federal governments. The municipalities thus find themselves at the mercy of these
higher levels of government and their legislative
bodies to obtain the added resources required just to
maintain the status quo.

At the same time, the service needs of the poor
outrace the input of resources from the higher levels
of government. This not only causes the poor to suffer, but both they and the city as a whole also lose
their capacity to determine how even these limited
resources will be used. In fact, the very resources
allocated from higher levels of government sometimes
have the ironic effect of hurting the very poor they
were intended to help. A few examples will illustrate this ironic state of affairs. Urban renewal
has brought economic benefits to the middle and upper
classes at the expense of reducing the already limited
housing available to the poor. Most of the early renewal projects had as their aim the revitalization of
the economic health of the city's central business district. The least economic properties, the slum housing
of the poor adjacent to the business district, were
cleared. Instead of low-income housing being built
to replace these units, the poor found themselves
competing for fewer units of equally substandard
housing for which they generally paid a higher rent.
On the cleared land, office buildings, shopping malls,
hotels, and middle-income and luxury apartments were
built, all of which benefited the more affluent owners and their clientele. Thus, the poor paid a high
social and economic cost while the affluent benefited.
In another instance, the $2 million transportation
bonds issued by the State of New York will do more
to provide an efficient rapid transit system for the
suburban and outlying middle-class residents to get
to work in New York City than it will to assist the
residents from the ghetto areas to move to the training opportunities and jobs that exist in the suburbs.
Finally, long-term FHA guaranteed loans have encouraged the rapid movement of the middle class to the
suburbs. The cost to the poor of this middle-class
benefit has been to lower the capacity of the city
to provide the tax dollars to pay for the services
needed by them.

Thus, the fiscal inability of the cities to renew themselves has the consequences of: (1) locking
the poor into their depressed conditions; (2) eroding
the cities' control over allocating funds that are
received from higher levels of government; and (3)
forcing the cities to accept new state and federal
programs that often improve the conditions of the
more affluent residents at the expense of the poor.

Shift in Family Structure

Another major historical trend that has affected
the condition of the poor is the shift in the nature
of the family structure from an extended family,
based on a rural economy, to a nuclear one, without
a compensating increase in public or private services
needed to meet their needs. The nuclear family is
an independent grouping that must rely on its own immediate members to do the many things that were formerly performed by aunts, uncles, and grandparents
in the extended family. Unable to fend for themselves
in times of crisis, the low-income nuclear family must
usually turn to the city services which have grown up
as proxies for the services formerly rendered by the
members of the extended family. For example, illness
of the mother may require a visiting nurse, a public
homemaker, and a welfare worker to insure the care of
family members and to guarantee payment for these
services. In the past, these responsibilities were
performed within the structure of the extended family.
The shift in family patterns has consequently placed
the poor more at the mercy of a depersonalized bureaucracy.

Furthermore, the manner in which these usually
inadequate services have been rendered to the poor has
often been alien to their needs. The poor find it
difficult having to wait for hours in a health clinic
for a few minutes with a busy, impersonal doctor. They
find it insulting to talk about their personal problems with social workers who seem indifferent to their
needs or react in a professionally impersonal manner.
They find it degrading to be told how to spend their
meager welfare check by welfare workers who know little about their cultural or personal habits. Because

of such indignities, the poor have consequently used
such public and voluntary services mainly as resources of last resort and generally in a family crisis. This condition has served to intensify and
make less manageable the nuclear family's capacity
to take care of itself and move out of poverty when
opportunities, few as they may be, have opened to it.
Thus, a mother would be prevented from entering a
training program by not having a family member to
watch her children, as might have been the case in
an extended family environment. Even in today's more
favorable conditions for assisting the poor, the in-
sufficiency of the services needed to replace the
functions formerly performed by larger families has
created a locked-in system of poverty which prevents
the poor from taking advantage of the open doors to
upward mobility.

Effect of Protestant Ethic

A final factor that has played an important role
in the maintenance of poverty conditions is the Protestant ethic that the famous sociologist Max Weber
articulated so well. One of the implications of this
ethic in our current environment is that it is felt
that only the worthy poor have been helped by the
wealthier members of society, who have long maintained
the vast network of voluntary social services existing in our country. These worthy poor are people with
high moral principles and the motivation for self-
help, but lacking the financial and professional resources to capitalize on their natural emotional,
moral, and intellectual strengths. The worthy poor
were generally those who accepted their benefactor's
values as their own. All other poor were considered
to be immoral, dependent, and drudges on society.
They were thus not worthy of the helping hand the
wealthy extended to them. Consequently, these un-
worthy poor--and they were the vast majority of the
poor--had to reform their attitudes and behavior before they were worthy of help. Only the minimal services needed to sustain them were to be given and
these through the public trough. Since the wealthy
also had a major influence until recent years in determining the amount of taxes they would pay for such

programs, these programs received the minimal amount
of funds possible. And the vast majority of the poor
who relied upon these services for assistance suffered as a result.

This "Protestant ethic" mentality, though losing
some of its force, still represents a potent influence in determining how much public revenue will be
directed at assisting the poor. This has been most
recently evidenced by the Congressional decision to
cut back $6 million from the federal budget in order
to pay for the Vietnam war and shore up our unbalanced economic system. Some of the cutback has come
from funds allocated to programs for the poor. It
has been evidenced by the grudging agreement of Congress to continue the anti-poverty program and to
finance the Model Cities program at a level too low
to bring about meaningful change. On the state level,
it has been evidenced by a recent drastic cutback in
New York State's medical program for the poor. The
practice of this ideology has thus become a major underlying cause of why our cities are in a state of
continued poverty. It has offered the affluent American a rationale for denying increased voluntary and
tax contributions to the urban poor.

While there may be other significant causes that
offer partial explanations for the distressed conditions of our cities, at least those presented here
represent some of the important factors that must be
taken into account in any discussion of poverty. Our
poor in the suburban and rural communities suffer
just as much as those in the cities from such economic, social, and ideological causes. These combined
factors tend to reinforce each other and to foster
the severe nature of the city's poverty areas. The
next section will identify how these causes have had
their impact on a prototype family living in poverty
conditions.

THE QUANTITATIVE AND QUALITATIVE ASPECTS
OF URBAN POVERTY

There are two aspects of poverty that must be taken
into account, the quantitative and the qualitative.

The quantitative aspect refers to the deficiencies
that exist in the decaying parts of the urban complex compared to the median benefits, opportunities,
and services available to the typical residents of
the metropolitan area. This study will not go into
a statistical analysis of these differences because
the statistics are not usually valid, accurate, or
current. They can be gained from any number of
studies that have been written to show the differences between sub-communities within our cities and
between the cities and the suburbs.

A hypothetical family will be used to illustrate
the impact that inadequate public resources have in
keeping a family in poverty. This is not a typical
family, but the problems described are those suffered
by many living in poverty areas. The first section
will focus on the detrimental effects these deficiencies have on the family. The second section will then
move to a discussion of the qualitative aspects of
poverty. While there may be some duplication in these
two discussions, this will merely serve the purpose
of emphasis and illustrate how interrelated the quantitative and qualitative aspects of poverty really are.

Impact of Inadequate Services on the
Lives of the Poor

Work

Mr. Jones, a 35-year-old married father of three
children, aged 12, 9, and 8, works as a janitor in a
nearby church of which he is a member. He earns $60
per week for the 40 weeks he annually works, there
being no need for his services in the summer. He sup-
plements his $2,400 per year income with odd jobs,
such as painting houses, cleaning up after special social gatherings, or working as a driver's assistant
delivering bulky packages. His total income is about
$3,500 per year. After spending $70 per month for
rent, $20 for heat and electricity, and $160 for food,
he has very little left for clothing, medical care,
entertainment, or buying necessary household items.

Trying to improve his income, he went to the State
Employment Office on several occasions to see about a

better-paying job, but none were available. Then
he responded to a leaflet that was left at his door
telling him of a new job-training program for persons
in circumstances like his. He consequently went to
the nearby manpower office as directed, where he was
tested and found to have a fifth-grade reading level.
This was too low for him to be eligible for the
better-paying training slots, which required an
eighth-grade education. He therefore agreed to join
a special class to upgrade his education. After four
months of this special tutoring, he had improved
enough to be eligible for training as a heavy-duty
truck driver, something that especially appealed to
him and for which he had an aptitude. However, he
learned that the neighborhood manpower center's quota
of five for that training course was filled, with
about twenty other eligible applicants waiting their
turns before Mr. Jones, which meant a two-year wait
before his turn came. There were no other training
positions that either interested him or for which he
had an aptitude.

He consequently gave up, after this conscientious
beginning effort, and resigned himself to his low
level of living. When he fell far into debt trying
to make ends meet, he left home, forcing his wife
and three children onto the welfare rolls. Unknown
to the welfare worker, he made regular visits to his
wife and children. In addition to the $287 per month
the welfare department granted his family, he gave
her another $60 per month to help pay back bills and
ease her life. Their combined income was now about
$6,500 per year, but the expenses needed to maintain
two households did not permit much more financial
discretion in spending their income. And the question
can be raised whether it was worth having their family
life pulled apart. Furthermore, a court order was
filed ordering Mr. Jones to pay his family $80 per
month, but since his whereabouts were unknown to the
authorities, the welfare department continued to pay
the family the full amount, while Mr. Jones was
legally charged with deserting his family and subject
to fine and arrest if apprehended.

Mr. Jones had thus been frustrated from improving
his job skills because of an inadequately funded

manpower program that was designed to cater especially to his type of problem, and his educational handi-
cap prevented his taking advantage of the traditional
services offered through the State Employment Office.
Faced with the prospect of going even deeper into
debt and eventually being dispossessed of his home
furnishings and other items of value, he chose the
only way open to him--deserting his family so they
could benefit from welfare assistance, which grant
approximated his earnings. He paid the consequences
for his act by gaining a criminal record and breaking
up his relationship with his family.

Housing

The Jones family was faced with the further problem that their $70 rent only permitted them to afford
an old, run-down apartment in a poor part of the city.
The four rooms permitted some privacy for the parents,
but none for the children, who were always in each
other's way and had no place to hang their clothes or
keep their possessions away from each other. They
were fortunate in having their own kitchen and bath-
room, but hot water was uncertain, the rooms were
cold and drafty in the winter, and the heat was suf-
focating in the summer. Although the building code
called for a minimum degree of heat during the cold
days, the absentee landlord preferred paying fines to
fixing the heating system if his tenants complained.
Those who complained had their rents raised so high
that they were forced to move. The tenants consequently were fearful of reporting the numerous housing violations: the broken windows; the fallen
ceiling plaster; or the broken glass that was still
on the hall stairs. Although Mrs. Jones had felt some
responsibility in the past to sweep her hall and
stairs, the failure of other neighbors to do so and
the indifference of the landlord made her apathetic
to shouldering her responsibility. She even lost
interest in trying to keep the children from their
active games that sometimes resulted in breaking light
bulbs in the corridors, or knocking out a weak railing
post as they tryed to outdo each other in wrestling
or pushing and shoving. They had no place to play
in their small apartment, nor was there any recreation center nearby.

Although the Jones children were careful not to break anything when they first moved in, they became less inhibited as they noted the greater freedom their mother gave them. In time, they stopped being concerned at all. Each time the landlord came for his rent, he made his quick inspections of his property and found more and more little bits of damage to it. He decided to get whatever profit he could out of it and do as little as possible to keep it in any semblance of proper maintenance. He reasoned that the families did not care so he saw little reason for caring either. The vicious cycle became worse in the Jones family when Mr. Jones left the home to live elsewhere and they went on welfare. Now, the mother was depressed more of the time, and the children simply did whatever they wished.

Mrs. Jones' welfare worker tried to help her find a better apartment, but there were no decent apartments available in neighborhoods with more disciplined children that were within her welfare budget. Besides, being black, she was forbidden by discriminatory practices from living in many parts of the city. Although she was opposed to living in the large impersonal housing projects, where she learned that things were almost as bad, she let the welfare worker make an application for her. To her dismay, she found that the waiting list was so long that it would take a year or more to gain admission. She consequently resigned herself to living amid the noise, the squalor, and the stench of her cramped apartment, which was deteriorating more rapidly each month.

Safety

When the Jones family had moved onto the block three years before, there had been occasional fights and some petty thievery reported, but it seemed that in the last year things were getting worse. When her 12-year-old son dashed in one day, slammed the door, and leaned heavily against it for a moment to hear if anyone was chasing after him, she learned that he had just stolen a purse from an elderly women whom he refused to identify. Although she scolded him and tried to make him return it--she learned it contained the

woman's welfare check--he refused and almost challenged his mother to make him. Mrs. Jones did not
know that her son was experimenting with drugs, had
cut classes very frequently, and had been given social promotions the last two years. She had tried
to believe that he was studying his lessons at a
friend's home. She had simply lost her ability to
communicate with him. When Mr. Jones made his periodic "secret" visits to the home, he tried talking
to his son, but it seemed to make no difference. He
had simply learned to go his own way and depend on
his relationship with his gang for guidance and
friendship. It became the most important reference
group in his life.

Police came onto the block only when a serious
crime had been committed and occasionally a patrol
car drove through the block, but it never stopped.
The people did not know the police on the beat nor
did the police know who the tenants were. A gang of
teenagers emerged as the controlling faction on the
block. They learned when people were away for the
day or taken to the hospital and simply made the
empty apartment their clubhouse until the tenant was
about to return. They took what they wanted and felt
impervious to potential punishment from either the
police or the neighbors who were too fearful of stop-
ping them. If a neighbor did call, the police were
usually too busy on other "emergencies" and the
neighbor might be found beaten the next day or his
apartment robbed. Mrs. Jones was no more safe walk-
ing the streets at night than were her neighbors.
She stopped going to the evening church meetings
where her husband had worked or to visit her only
friend two blocks away. She reduced her social contacts and spent more of her time at home, where she
became even more preoccupied with her sad plight in
life.

Thus, as the property deteriorated and the rents
were lowered to entice tenants, a poorer and more disadvantaged class of people moved in, accelerating an
already worsened situation. The social controls that
were normally provided by neighbors who look after
each other are limited in areas dominated by families

in the poverty cycle. When, furthermore, because of
limited tax resources, secondary social controls provided by public servants such as the police, truant
officers, or clergy are unable to make up for these
neighborhood deficiencies, then the law of the jungle
takes over with the strong dominating the weak. The
police, whose salaries are largely paid by the property and business owners, generally respond to their
calls for help. Since most police forces are inadequately staffed, this effectively limits the amount
of police protection available to those residing in
the poverty areas.

Health

Mrs. Jones was so concerned about her shattered
family life that one day she absentmindedly cut her
finger while dicing some carrots. She severed a
blood vessel. Not having a band-aid, she simply
washed out the cut with cold water and wrapped it
with an old piece of rag she had handy. In time, the
blood stopped running, but she paid no attention to
the bandage. The next day, when her finger turned
blue and pained a little, she went to the corner
drugstore to call her social worker to find out what
she could do to get medical attention. She lost her
three dimes trying to get the busy line, and the op-
erator would not convey a message for her. There
were no doctors in the neighborhood, but she asked
the druggist what she could do. He advised her to
soak the finger and then see a doctor, because he
saw it was infected. The only place she could get
medical attention was at the emergency room of the
municipal hospital, but she had sworn never to return
there when, several years ago, she had to wait standing with her two small children for almost five hours
to get service. When she had finally seen a doctor,
he had given her some medicine for her stomach ail-
ment and told her to come back in two weeks. And he
charged her for the visit, as her husband was still
living with her at the time and she was not receiving
welfare assistance. The long walk to a first bus and
then the wait to transfer to a second bus to get to
the clinic made the trip back and forth for five minutes of a busy, indifferent doctor's time hardly wort

a second effort. But her finger pained more and
made her feel ill. She only had a dollar left and
could not afford a taxi, even if she were lucky enough
to find one. She went home and decided to soak it and
then try to reach the welfare worker again the next
day.

Overnight, her whole arm became swollen and she
was in dire pain when she woke up the next day. When
she fainted as she tried to cook breakfast after
dressing and washing, her younger daughter rushed out
of the house to get her brother, who stole somebody's
car to drive her to the municipal hospital. She was
immediately hospitalized and given emergency treatment which luckily resulted in only the loss of the
infected finger. But during her recuperation period,
the three children had to fend for themselves for
several days before the social worker learned about
the situation from the hospital. Mrs. Jones received
adequate attention during the initial phase of her
hospitalization, but saw the doctor only once from
the third to the seventh day, when she was released
a few days "early" because the bed was needed by another patient. During this seven-day stay in the
hospital, the social worker was unable to locate a
homemaker to venture into that neighborhood or stay
overnight with the children. To protect the children
during the absence of an adult, she decided to place
them in an emergency foster home until their mother's
return; but the teenage boy simply disappeared, so
that only the two girls were housed in a foster home.

When Mrs. Jones returned home, too weakened to
care for herself, a visiting nurse did make a visit
every other day for a week, but the main burden of
running the house fell on the two young girls after
they were returned from their foster home. They managed to get by somehow, but Mrs. Jones' weakness and
loss of a finger further depressed her so that she
had even less will to take care of things. Although
Mr. Jones learned of his family's plight, he was too
fearful of returning to the house to watch the children for fear of being apprehended and jailed for
non-support of his family. He had been away almost
a year now and was gradually seeing his wife and

children less frequently. Mrs. Jones was usually
too tired and depressed to have sexual relations with
him and seemed to complain all the time about the
children. He consequently found companionship elsewhere and began diverting some of the money he was
giving to the family to maintain his new social relationship. This loss of financial support further
deepened the troubles of the family.

Education

Mrs. Jones had three children in school. The
teenage boy was in the sixth grade, having repeated
one grade and been given social promotions in his
last two years. When the family was united, his
mother, who could read at the eighth-grade level, encouraged his reading and he enjoyed the attention he
received then. But, his two younger sisters, also
looking for attention, would take his books and look
at the pictures and sometimes tear the pages acciden-
tally. Once the teacher scolded him for this so he
stopped bringing books home from school and began
looking at comic books instead. He had no quiet place
to read in the home and the pull of the other children
on him to join a gang they had formed was pretty
strong. At school, he found the teacher catering to
a half-dozen of the smarter children while largely
ignoring him and many others like him. He could not
keep up with the pace of the teacher's plan that
called for specified progress in certain subject areas
each week. He seldom handed in the few homework assignments given him and eventually lost interest in
what happened in the class.

He found more interest and challenge in the activities of his gang than he did in school. He consequently fooled around in class and became disruptive
to the teacher's effort to control the class and give
her attention to those trying to learn. He often
found himself being reprimanded by the principal.
Finding himself restless and frustrated in school, he
cut his classes more frequently. And after his father
left the home, he did pretty much as he pleased, going
to school when he felt like it.

Mrs. Jones' two daughters, meantime, were in the second and third grades. One was especially bright, likable, and was given special attention by the teacher; the other was average, did well in the subjects she liked, but poorly in those that were more difficult for her. The result was that the bright girl advanced with the best students, while the normal child began to fall behind in her reading and arithmetic. Mrs. Jones could not help her in either of these subjects, but did encourage both her daughters to do good work. The teachers had one conference with Mrs. Jones concerning her brighter child, but none concerning her son or other daughter. Although encouraged by the teacher, she could not afford to buy her children the extra books, paints, or recordings they might have enjoyed, or the bus fare for the class trips.

Although the school had a parent-teachers organization, Mrs. Jones was too tired or busy at night to attend. The one time her husband was home to watch the children, she went and found only a few parents and teachers present, so she decided not to make the effort to go again. She was especially annoyed that none of her children's teachers were in attendance as she wanted to talk to them about their progress. After her husband left home, her increased depression made it more difficult for her to pay much attention to the school activities of the children. She was often irritable with the girls and shouted at them for help in the home.

The one time Mrs. Jones was able to talk to her brighter daughter's teacher, she learned how difficult it was for the teacher to keep her class of thirty active students under control. She felt frustrated at being unable to give the attention she desired to all of the children. She found herself working especially hard with the best, most alert students and giving whatever time was left over to the others. Her school had no social workers or psychologists to work with the more difficult children and she did not have the time either during class or after school to give them the personal attention they needed. She was too busy

attending a number of school meetings and working on
other administrative assignments.

She would have liked an assistant or two and more
audio-visual equipment and material. The classroom,
designed for 25 students, was too small for the 30
children she had. Whenever papers were passed out or
any movement took place, minor commotions erupted as
children bumped into others trying to get past them.
The arguments and bickerings among them were as much
the result of their being jostled as it was the slow-
er, more frustrated and bored students' way of finding
an outlet for their dammed-up energies. Although the
teacher understood all of this, she felt helpless to
do anything about it. She had told Mrs. Jones that
she was requesting a transfer to another school where
the classes were smaller and the conditions for teach
ing were more conducive. She realized that apathy
was overtaking her when she found she was dragging
herself to school each day and trying to leave as
quickly as possible after school. All of her initial
enthusiasm that so energized the students in her firs
year at the school three years ago had drained away.
She realized part of the class apathy to learning was
a response to her own indifference, except for the
chosen few upon whom she lavished her attention.
Knowing this was unfair to the majority of the class,
she wanted to transfer to a new school. Furthermore,
the school was old and dreary and there was little
effort to provide after-school activities for the
children.

Thus, the overwork, the difficulty in communicat-
ing with children who brought so much frustration and
inertia from home, the lack of facilities and equipment conducive to learning, and the inadequate support
ive services, most of which were available in the better parts of town, conspired to make the learning and
teaching processes very difficult to manage for both
the teachers and the students. Although the schools
took the largest portion of the city budget, the tax
revenues were not sufficient to replace the old
schools, reduce the size of classes, or initiate new
programs except in those areas most ready for them.
These were usually in the middle- or upper-income

residential sections of the city. And since representatives from these areas sat on the Board of Education and the teachers and school administrators
lived in these neighborhoods, it was only natural
that they would favor the people with whom they most
closely identified and who in turn responded favorably to their efforts. The desires of the teachers
in the low-income areas to transfer to the higher-
income areas was further evidence for the decision-
makers not to squander the public tax dollar in areas
where the children either were not learning or did
not care to learn. The result was that the more affluent segments of the population were favored over
the poorer parts of town, and this only widened the
disparity between the two groups.

This series of graphic illustrations makes the
point of what can happen and has happened to a family
caught in the throes of poverty. These are only symptoms that are brought about by some of the underlying
causes of poverty discussed earlier. The Protestant
ethic that favors the motivated over the apathetic,
the use of limited public revenues to benefit the more
affluent over the poorer segments of the population,
the incapacity of public resources to make up for the
deficiencies of private services in the poverty areas,
the almost total absence of representatives of the
poor to the city-wide centers where decisions are made
in resource allocations, and the generally negative
attitude by the dominant decision-makers and the people they represent toward the poor; all of these are
causes which cumulatively reinforce and maintain poor
families in their poverty spiral.

The poor consequently suffer from an inequality
of opportunity, service, and benefits compared to the
typical urban family. The public and private resources
made available up to this time to deal with these comprehensive problems have provided palliatives rather
than permitting the enactment of real measures that
can reverse the downward spiral of poverty. Let us
now turn to a discussion of some of the qualitative
aspects of poverty that tend to further aggravate attempts to cope with the problem.

Qualitative Aspects of Poverty

Family Tensions

In the first place, the poor have a high degree
of family tensions. Some of these tensions arise
from their inadequate financial resources and the instability of their family structure. A large number
of poor rely on public welfare assistance. Most of
these are families with a single parent or elderly pe
sons living alone. The single parent with children
especially has a difficult time maintaining disciplin
over the lives of active, demanding children. Discipline can break down when the emotional resources
of a spouse and the economic margin of comfort to
provide the basic and discretional material things a
family and a home need are absent. When all the othe
services required are also lacking (homemakers, nursing service, police protection, or a nearby doctor),
then even the substitute measures the average family
takes for granted tend to reinforce the sense of family disorganization and heighten tension. This in
turn breeds a feeling of apathy and an attitude of
indifference at the behavior and actions of the children, who then tend to run their own lives.

There appear to be several reasons for this increased tension. One of these is the change in the fa
ily pattern so that the nuclear family, especially
the poor, is dependent on governmental and private
social services in periods of family crisis. In the
case of the welfare family, the attitude of the general population and its elected officials tends to
reflect the Protestant ethic. This results in the
provision of only minimal tax support for needed public services. Finally, the high mobility rate of bot
the general population and the poor tends to reduce
reliance on close informal relationships that would
have ordinarily taken up the slack resulting from a
change in the family structure.

Alienation

A second qualitative factor that affects the poor
especially is a sense of alienation that pervades

people in all economic levels. This alienation is
manifested in the phrase, "You can't fight city hall."
The apathy expressed in this phrase is especially
true of the poor who feel even further removed from
the seats of power. In recent years, however, the
hostility that underlies this sense of helplessness
has welled to the surface. Both individual and collective acts of violence have rapidly increased. The
alienation of the poor has turned its collective
anger against the custodians of the public system:
the police, teachers, social workers, non-resident
store owners and landlords. This collective hostility
is as dangerous to the residents in the poverty areas
as it is to those living outside them. However, a
number of studies have shown that most of the anger
has been turned inward, against those living in the
slums rather than against the indifferent average
American living outside the poverty areas. This has
taken the forms of sporadic riots, burning and looting of homes and stores, increased crimes against
those poor least able to defend themselves, crime
arising from addicts, and an increase in the number
of rapes and acts of prostitution. Recent New York
City precinct crime rates have shown that the more a
precinct suffers from conditions of poverty, the
higher the crime rate. Thus, individual hostility
in the form of petty crimes and collective hostility
in the form of riots and ugly demonstrations are far
more prevalent in the slums than in the average urban
neighborhood. Although the emphasis in recent discussions has placed the "safety in the streets" slogan
as one of the key issues concerning Americans, it is
an issue that has affected the poor more than the
average American. The fear that the crimes of the
poor against themselves may point outward to become
crimes against the average American made this a major
political issue in the 1968 election campaigns.

The causes of this alienation and concomitant
heightened hostility are a sense of powerlessness and
a need to lash out violently against the faceless bureaucracy, the system, that holds the poor in poverty.
It is through this direct thrust at the fountain of
power that the poor, and especially the blacks, are
affirming their own identity and sense of unity to
overcome this alienation.

Citizen Participation

Until recent years, the poor have participated
minimally in the decisions of those public and private service agencies and clubs whose services have
so vitally affected them. They have therefore had
less to say about the kind of education, police protection, sanitation services, welfare assistance, or
medical treatment they received than those living in
better neighborhoods. The great burdens that over-
power a single-parent family and the resulting family
disorganization and lowered discipline over children'
activity have permitted too little time for such parents to join PTA's, Leagues of Women Voters, hospital volunteer groups, political clubs, boys clubs,
boards of voluntary social agencies, and other such
groups.

However, the black's struggle for equal rights
and the federal government's "war on poverty" have
begun to change this lowered degree of citizen participation. The social, psychological, economic, and
cultural environment of the poor has colored the form
their involvement has taken. Debates that lead to
putting off concrete results have a lower priority
than direct action in the form of sit-ins, marches,
threats, physical violence, and demands for changes
now. The great urgency for action, the autocratic
rule of a few strong-willed ethnic leaders, the militancy of the demands, and the emotional fervor with
which the poor make decisions are in sharp contrast
to the more subdued, almost passive, time-delaying
and time-consuming discussions which characterize
most of the typical American forms of citizen involvement. It is this very difference in the way the two
forms of citizen activity have taken shape that is
most disconcerting to both sides. It helps explain
why the typical American describes changes in the effort to help the Negro and other poverty groups as
being "too fast," while the minority groups describe
them as being "too slow." Yet, as of this writing,
in spite of the public attention given to the gains
of the poor in citizen involvement, the reins of power
still remain very much in the hands of the white
decision-makers.

Discrimination

Another qualitative factor that prevents the poor
from achieving parity with the typical American is
discrimination. The most prominent characteristic of
this discrimination is related to color. From a
sense of guilt about his black skin, the Negro is beginning to identify with his blackness with a feeling
of pride. From this, the concept of "black power"
has arisen as a rallying cry for the Negro. Black
culture, black ownership of economic power, black
political power, and black dress are only a few of
the forms embraced by the concept of "black power."
Yet, this emphasis on "black power," while a powerful
and beneficial rallying cry for the blacks among the
poor, has had an unsettling and sometimes fearsome
effect among average Americans. Instead of seeing
it as the blacks' way to counteract discrimination
toward them and to achieve a more rapid parity with
the average American, the whites view this effort as
a form of "reverse discrimination." Instead of parity,
many whites fear the loss of jobs, status, and opportunity they have enjoyed for so many years without
competition from the blacks. This new source of competition for the whites has set up conditions of conflict between the two groups. And the whites' great
concern at this competition strongly implies that
discrimination by color is beginning to break down.

However, there are other forms of discrimination
that continue to resist change and in effect require
the massive structural changes and new resource of a
Model Cities program, namely, institutional discrimination. This is most evidenced by a double standard
of services: a lower quality for the poor and higher
quality for the more affluent. The poor have access
only to poor, ineffective public schools; the more
affluent to better-run public schools and high-quality
private schools. The poor have access to a low standard of public social services; the more affluent to
professional social services provided by private welfare agencies. The poor must rely almost exclusively
on inaccessible, low-grade municipal hospitals for
medical care; the more affluent have access to nearby
private doctors, group medical services and high-quality

non-profit hospitals. The double standard is evident
in almost every aspect of the institutions that serve
both populations. This type of discrimination is so
deeply rooted in the structure of our American institutional system that basic changes would be required to make it more responsive to the poor's needs
and ways of using services. Until such changes do
occur, the present system represents the more serious
form of discrimination which inhibits the opening up
of opportunities of service and jobs to the poor.

While there may be other quantitative and qualitative characteristics that could be discussed, these
are the more prominent ones that help identify the
nature of poverty as it exists in the urban areas today. Let us now examine some of the federal legislative attempts to cope with some of the conditions
discussed in this chapter.

LEGISLATIVE ATTEMPTS TO COPE WITH POVERTY

Since 1949, the year the first major postwar
piece of social legislation was passed to do something
about the human and physical problems accumulating in
the cities, a number of significant legislative acts
have been passed. These federal acts have been of
two types: those that have been addressed to structural changes in the way our system works; and those
that have brought new and expanded services to the
cities.

Structural Governmental Changes

Although no detailed discussion will be made here
of the structural changes, a passing reference ought
to be made to the more significant of these. Among
these have been the creation of two new federal departments: the Department of Health, Education, and
Welfare; and that of Housing and Urban Development.
Both have since undergone internal structural changes
in an attempt to find the best administrative mix to
make them more effective and efficient in dealing with
their problem areas. In addition, an executive department, the Office of Economic Opportunity, was
created which had independent resources and has acted

as a catalyst to change the directions of the traditional federal departments. This office has been
responsible for our current "war on poverty." Another new important office, that of Model Cities, was
established within the Department of Housing and Urban
Development. It has been charged with coordinating
the massive federal resources currently going into
the cities. The final structural change that has
taken place has geen the direct grants-in-aid made by
the federal government to the cities, thereby bypass-
ing the state governments. This has been done in the
urban renewal program, the anti-poverty program and,
most recently, in the Model Cities program.

The primary aim of these structural changes has
been to make the federal government more responsive
to the needs of the municipal officials and the problems confronting them. The continuing changes that
have taken place indicate that this is an evolving
process for which there is no final solution. The
increasing magnitude of the urban problem indicates
that none of these structural efforts by themselves
have had a major influence on either reducing or con-
taining the problems facing the poor and the cities.

Federal Program Changes

More important even than the structural changes
that have occurred are the program changes. Those
that will be discussed here are as follows:

(1) Federal Housing Act of 1949;
(2) 1954 Amendments to the Federal Housing
     Act of 1949;
(3) Public Welfare Amendments of 1962;
(4) The Community Mental Health Centers Act
     of 1963;
(5) Economic Opportunity Act of 1964;
(6) Elementary and Secondary Education Act
     of 1965;
(7) Health Insurance Amendments to the Social
     Security Act of 1966; and
(8) Demonstration Cities and Metropolitan
     Development Act of 1966.

There have been other important legislative acts
including manpower training, civil rights, and hospital construction programs. The purpose of discussing the above acts is mainly to illustrate the federal government's method of dealing with urban
problems. The listing of these acts points to two con-
clusions. First, the federal government is placing
more resources in the hands of the cities at a rapidly increasing pace. The great majority of legislative
changes affecting cities have been enacted after 1960.
Thus, the federal government has assumed increasing
responsibility for what happens in the cities.

Second, the federal government has directed its
efforts at a widening spectrum of urban problems.
However, these efforts have been on a piecemeal,
problem-oriented basis. A mental-health problem required legislation dealing with only mental health;
job training with preparing the poor for jobs, and so
forth. It was not until the passage of the Economic
Opportunity Act of 1964 that governmental legislation
encompassed more than one problem area at a time.
The Model Cities Act is the most recent and comprehensive attempt at dealing with a wide scope of urban
problems.

The Federal Housing Act of 1949

The Federal Housing Act of 1949 was a major break-
through on the part of Congress in trying to provide
decent housing for every family, while using the concept of urban renewal to begin the rebuilding of our
decaying cities. In this approach it was hoped that
social, physical, and economic goals would be interrelated and lead to the rebirth of our cities. It
did not quite work out that way. Housing was built
for the middle- and upper-income families while the
poor were pushed deeper into the already overcrowded
ghettos. Congress reacted to these negative consequences to the poor by amending the Housing Act in
1954 to require the municipalities to meet federal
guidelines set down in a workable seven-point program.
This beginning emphasis on citizen participation and
the taking into account of the needs of the residents
being displaced led to a more humane city rebuilding

program. Yet, the program still continued to emphasize the rebirth of the central business districts
and the construction of high-priced apartment housing
which the poor could not afford. While the relocation
of the poor was made more humane, there still existed
too little "safe and standard" apartments to house
those displaced by the urban renewal projects.

As a consequence, the program took on new empha-
ses. First, rehabilitation and construction of residential housing for the poor replaced the total
land-clearance emphasis. Second, the poor demanded
and received a greater voice in the planning of their
neighborhoods. But, in spite of all the accumulated
wisdom gained by those who advocated the physical rebirth of the cities, there were other critics who
pointed out that the housing programs did little to
rehabilitate the people who lived in these slums.

The 1962 Public Welfare Amendments

With the coming of the Kennedy administration,
Congress addressed itself to many of the social problems that so concerned the poor. The welfare system
was especially vulnerable to criticism because it
was held responsible for offering a bare subsistence
level to the poor without doing anything to offer the
services needed to help break the "poverty cycle."
The 1962 Public Welfare Amendments recognized this
deficiency by providing matching federal dollars to
encourage the states to offer a wide range of social
services to help the welfare recipient out of poverty. Unfortunately, the provision of these services
was not mandatory and their cost was very high. But,
more important, the professional doctors, nurses,
social workers, and vocational counselors were not
available in sufficient numbers to render the services
even if the funds were available. The result was that
the states gave little emphasis to the service aspect
of the welfare system so that few profited by the
meager restorative services that were offered. Yet,
it is questionable if the spending of more money
would have made any difference, because those on welfare suffered from such a wide variety of disabilities
over which the welfare system had little control.

The Community Mental Health Centers Act of 1963

Among the disabled on welfare were the mentally
ill and mentally retarded. The Community Mental
Health Centers Act of 1963 recognized that the lot
of those suffering from these illnesses was not improved by shutting them away in the dim, isolated,
and sometimes walled bastions that passed for hospitals. There they received little care and had to
learn to adjust to a life away from normal society.
As with welfare, those with these illnesses rose in
number so that more hospitals had to be built just
to hold them in custody. A new generation of psychiatric caretakers argued strenuously that the mentally
ill could better be helped in their own communities
and homes by catching the symptoms of illnesses at
their incipient stage and by providing a full comple-
ment of services in the community. By bringing the
family of the ill person into the circle of those
seeking to help the mentally disabled, it was reasoned
that not only could the person get well quicker but
his readjustment to his normal routine of life would
be speeded up if he were treated in the community.
Congress consequently provided heavy sums of money
in 1963 to build community mental health centers where
the mentally ill and retarded could be treated. A
few years later, it also provided funds for the training and hiring of the psychiatric personnel required
to treat them. It is too early to evaluate the results of such a major new program. But it is not too
early to recognize that the rehabilitation of the mentally ill will not succeed without at the same time
providing them with the job training and educational
skills required to return them to a productive life.

The Elementary and Secondary Education Act of 1965

Although a general focus on the state of our
educational system was made following the Russians'
first flight into outer space in the late 1950's, it
was not until civic leaders, educators, and legislators began to examine the education of our children
in the cities and especially in the low-income areas
that the real impact began to be felt. It became
evident that our educational system was in a state of

disarray. Schools were old and overcrowded. Classrooms were unmanageable and were more often expensive
baby-sitting services rather than places for stimu-
lation of the mind and senses of the children. Some
blamed the professional schools of higher education
for not focusing on the special needs of the low-
income and urban children. Others blamed the dreary
and squalid environment which appeared almost hostile
to those who passed through the school doors on a
daily basis. Some blamed the teachers for not being
more innovative and simply giving up in their efforts
to stimulate the minds of the poor to learn. Others
blamed the movement of the wealthier families into
the suburbs for lowering the quality of education in
the inner cities, segregating the children and pre-
venting the cities from paying for the increased
costs of education. As a result of these accumulated
pressures, Congress finally acted, after several
years of debate, by passing the Elementary and Secondary Education Act of 1965.

This act acknowledged the imbalance of funds allocated for educating the poor against those for the
middle-class child who lived in the wealthier suburbs. Consequently, special financial assistance was
granted for the education of children of low-income
families. In addition, funds were granted to upgrade
the deficient libraries and to provide for experimentation with new course offerings and other educational
material designed to stimulate the education process
of children living in our urban slums. Finally,
funds were set aside to provide for educational, Rand-
type "think tanks" where new ideas, research, and
demonstrations could take place to assist the poor
specifically, and education in general. These federal
inputs of large sums of funds have materially aided
the cities to begin rebuilding their old school plants,
while infusing new ideas into the curriculum and preparing teachers to work with low-income children and
their families.

The 1965 Health Insurance Amendments

At the same time this battle was being fought,
another battle was being waged and won. Ever since

the passage of the Social Security Act in the early 1930's, a small band of citizens demanded that a comprehensive health system be established to insure proper medical services for every American. The American Medical Association and its allies were able to defeat repeated attempts to pass such legislation. The association feared such legislation would be the first step, as in England, toward government control of medicine and medical practitioners. However, the rising number of elderly, the rapidly increasing cost of medicine, and the retired person's inability to pay for such medical attention finally won the day with the passage of the Health Insurance Amendments to the Social Security Act in 1965. At the same time, a little-noticed amendment also provided for eventual mandatory health benefits to all families receiving welfare assistance or earning too little money to afford medical care. Thus, one of the chronic concerns of the poor, their inability to pay for private doctors and hospital bills, was somewhat mitigated by these far-reaching amendments.

The current concern in Congress is the adverse impact of the mounting cost of health services on the federal and state budgets. Instead of widening the benefits offered the elderly and the poor, more limited services are being offered or the income limits of eligibility are being reduced by both Congress and the state's enabling legislation. Nevertheless, because Congress has recognized the provision of adequate health services as a right for every American, it is unlikely that these benefits will be eliminated in the future.

The Economic Opportunity Act of 1964

In spite of all these individual efforts to attack various conditions that hold people in poverty, Congress felt that a more comprehensive and coordinated attack on poverty itself should be instituted. The passage of the Economic Opportunity Act of 1964 was the result. This was a far-ranging act that attempted to open the door wide to let cities do whatever they considered necessary to resolve the problem of poverty. Innovative demonstrations of all types

were encouraged. Emphasis was placed on the poor
themselves becoming involved in setting policies and
deciding on the type of programs they desired. Community action agencies were formed in thousands of
communities in the United States operated by the poor
themselves. Many of the initial efforts of the poor
were directed against the existing city agencies--
especially the welfare departments, schools, and employment offices--to change their practices and regulations. Where possible, competitive systems of
social welfare systems were established. The power
placed in the hands of the poor through the funneling
of anti-poverty funds directly into the poverty areas
threatened the traditional welfare, economic, and
political systems that had heretofore served the poor.
It was these very systems, however, that the Congress
felt were needed to join hands with the new, rising
poverty leaders to wipe out poverty. But this has
not happened. Too low funds, too high expectations,
and too little coordination at the local level have
frustrated the poor and increased their hostility
toward the "white" dominated power systems that have
continued to hold them down. Furthermore, it was
recognized that human renewal without simultaneous
physical renewal would not eradicate poverty. A total comprehensive approach was required. And this
meant a partnership of the poor with the private and
public leadership in the community. The Model Cities
program was conceived as the comprehensive antidote
to hopefully resolve the problems of the slums. Congress had begrudgingly recognized that every piecemeal
approach it had tried and the billions of dollars in
the individual programs it had created had not done
the job. Let us now turn to an examination of this
most comprehensive of all the federal efforts to
eradicate the poverty pockets of the cities.

THE MODEL CITIES PROGRAM

The program is designed to be carried out in two
stages. The first stage permits up to one year for
each municipality to plan a detailed one-year action
plan and to set comprehensive, five-year goals. The
first cities selected for this program divided $12

million to plan in the first year. Some $300 million
was also appropriated for the initial "supplemental"
funds to execute portions of the first-year plan.
These "supplemental" funds could be utilized for any
program the City Demonstration Agency (CDA) deemed
desirable and for which other sources of funds were
not available. It was expected that a detailed plan
would be worked out each year to move toward the objectives stated in the initial five-year plan. No
new planning funds would be made available after the
first year, but it was expected that such funds
could be used from the cost of administering the program to fund the planning of each succeeding year.

The act specifies four objectives of the program:

(1) Renew entire slum neighborhoods by com-
    bined use of physical and social
    development programs.
(2) Increase substantially the supply of
    standard housing of low and moderate
    cost.
(3) Make marked progress in reducing social
    and educational disadvantages, ill
    health, underemployment and enforced
    illness.
(4) Contribute toward a well-balanced city.

In order to plan and execute such objectives, the
CDA is expected to meet five criteria:

(1) The programs identified in the plan should
    be initiated quickly.
(2) The programs required the identification
    of the sources of funds to adequately
    implement the programs.
(3) The private sector should be fully in-
    volved in the planning and implementa-
    tion of the program.
(4) A relocation plan should be developed to
    assist those displaced by any of the
    programs.
(5) The program is required to be in keeping
    with the comprehensive plan for the
    entire urban and metropolitan area.

CDA Letter No. 3 additionally specified that the
local residents in the Model Cities neighborhoods
would be involved in the planning process and execution of the plan. Furthermore, the local administrative procedures that were spelled out should be
feasible for carrying out the program on a consoli-
dated and coordinated basis; and finally all agencies
and private concerns will have expressed their willingness to cooperate in the endeavors in which they
have an interest.

The plan must also include an evaluative proced-
ure whereby analyses of the costs and benefits of
alternative courses of action could be studied and
lead to recommended improvements in the programs.

These then are the major features of the act.
The design is grand, the objective laudable, and the
resources negligible. A study of CDA Letters No. 1
and 2 indicates that HUD is serious in its intent to
produce master plans that will lead to a substantial
reduction in the multi-faceted problems that combine
to produce our slums. But, the question remains
whether this planning process and the demands being
made on the CDAs are feasible. Some of the questions
can be raised in the context of what has occurred
thus far in the Model Cities program in New York City.

First, the real effectiveness of the CDA can be
achieved only if the cooperating agencies, city and
private, agree to give up some of their administrative
practices and controls in order to coordinate their
services. This appears to be an unrealistic demand
in the face of how the administrators of these agencies judge success and their personal progress. It
is one thing for an administrator of a major program
to cooperate by sitting around a table with other administrators to discuss problems and issues in weld-
ing programs together. It is another for that
administrator to also give up a portion of his program
staff or authority to insure the greater effectiveness
of the program in question. Cooperation does not
necessarily lead to coordination. Yet, those sitting
around the table claim their body is a coordinative
one. Thus, it is entirely possible for a local

community to meet with the "letter of the law," but
not its spirit. This issue will be examined more
closely in a later chapter.

There is also a conflict in the objectives of
planning programs that can be mounted quickly and the
involvement of citizen groups in the planning process.
HUD's Urban Renewal Agency has had much experience in
recognizing how slow-moving the planning process
really is when it involves citizens interacting with
city and private interests. Not only must the citizen representatives be educated to the resources
available, the use of professional staff, and the use
of demographic data, but also the whole question of
what their functions and powers of decision-making
are must be resolved. In New York City, New Haven,
and Hartford, this had been one of the key stumbling
blocks in creating a CDA board. Boston's experience
with citizen participation in the urban-renewal planning process revealed that none of its three major
neighborhood plans was completed in less than three
years. Lest one think this a problem only where the
residents of the low-income areas are involved, one
can cite numerous examples where even less-ambitious
planning has required several years to gain support
among different interest groups. For example, the
powerful thrust generated in New York City to decentralize its school system has been set back at least
two years by the actions of the state legislature.
Thus, it almost seems to be taken for granted that
planning will not be rapid and it is highly doubtful
if a single city will compete any kind of Model Cities
plan within the year allocated in the act and still
involve residents in meaningful planning.

The planning objectives call for the creation of
a five-year plan and a one-year program which can be
mounted quickly. This dual emphasis sets up a series
of dilemmas. The residents are less concerned with
setting five-year goals than they are with mounting
programs that can be implemented quickly--a goal of
the act, the mayors, Congress, and the poor. Mounting
programs quickly leads to emphasis on planning for
one year at a time rather than for five years all at
the same time. It leads to fragmented project

planning rather than comprehensive planning. It leads
to a continuation of status quo programs, which require mere expansion of current services, rather than
planning for innovative programs or systems of delivery, which require changing the system and/or drastically altering the existing programs. It leads
finally to a maintenance of control of the programs
in the hands of the existing "power" structure rather
than to an increase in the influence and power of the
Model Cities residents who participated in the planning process. In short, the emphasis on one aspect
of the planning objectives leads to negative consequences for the other.

A further conflict in the act's objectives is
between the desire of the act to utilize local residents in the rebuilding process and the emphasis on
maintaining cost efficiency by using new methods of
construction. It is unrealistic to expect that
unions, already having difficulty in providing steady
employment for their present members, will recruit
large numbers of Model Cities residents into their
apprenticeship programs and further jeopardize their
obligations to the current membership. Even if this
did happen, these apprenticeship programs are time-
consuming, running two years and more before a resident can be considered fully trained in his craft.
Thus, conflicts will occur between the resident poor
and the unions over job openings in the Model Cities
area under any circumstances. But, when the act also
encourages labor-saving construction techniques, this
can only exacerbate the already difficult objective
of providing jobs for the poor.

Another contradiction is becoming evident in the
first stages of the Model Cities program between the
very limited sums of "new" funds being made available
in relation to the nature of the real problem and the
emphasis on producing a comprehensive community plan.
Feasible planning leads to developing only those programs that can be funded by known sources of financial
resources. Since most of the funding sources are earmarked for known project areas and the percentage increase in expansion of funds for these projects is
generally on an incremental basis, feasible planning

dictates directing program objectives toward these
sources of incremental increases in funds. On this
basis, it does not make sense to those involved in
Model Cities planning to prepare plans for which funding is a highly uncertain possibility. In the recent
development of the Neighborhood Service Program, a
multi-service social welfare system in New York City,
the citizen committees and their planners took the fed
eral government at its word that funds would be made
available to implement programs suggested by the community. It soon developed that six to seven times
the amount of available resources would be required
to fund these programs. The time and effort, the
tensions and community arguments, the exacerbation of
already tense relationships between the city agencies
and the community planning groups were experiences
that will not be forgotten in New York City as the
Model Cities program begins its planning process.
Thus, the high expectations of the Model Cities program may well have to be diluted if the planning is
going to be guided by the availability of known resources.

These are only a few of the many dilemmas and
contradictions that will face the CDAs as they begin
planning for the Model Cities program. Yet, the intent of the program objectives merely underscore dilemmas which all communities have always had to face.
These are not new conflicts. They have existed over
numerous issues: city or community control of funds,
emphasis on efficiency or effectiveness, better housing at the expense of more housing, the needs of the
poor within the Model Cities areas versus the poor
living outside these neighborhoods, and funds for
schools versus funds for jobs or social services.
Choices from among numerous alternatives will have
to be made during planning. The issue is not whether
conflicts are inherent in the Model Cities objectives,
but rather whether there will be sufficient resources
made available to demonstrate whether, in fact, a comprehensive, coordinated attack on the conditions of th
poverty areas can make a difference. The piecemeal approach has failed. Will the Model Cities comprehensiv
approach also fail for other reasons, such as those
cited? The unrest generated by the aroused militant

demands of the poor, the outbreak of widespread
riots, and the Poor People's March on Washington have
all accentuated the necessity to make the Model Cities
program work.

A review of the causes and the nature of the conditions of the poverty areas suggests that even a
Model Cities program cannot resolve all the multi-
faceted problems that beset the poor. It may be impossible to transform a predominantly residential
neighborhood into a balanced community which can provide sufficient jobs, commercial centers, cultural
opportunities, as well as good residential neighborhoods. It may well be necessary to look to employment opportunities beyond the Model Cities areas to
meet this great need. Healthful, natural retreats
from the rigors of a fast-paced, crowded, neighborhood community may well require the buying of land
for a camp in the hills and woods outside the city.
It may be too expensive and inefficient to build a
hospital in a Model Cities area. And this decision
may well require a flexible and inexpensive transportation system to connect the residents to these hospitals. It may not be possible to meet the strong
national trend of housing people in single-family
homes with their own private yards in the model
neighborhoods. Nor is it likely that any single
model community could be made so diversified in the
type of housing, jobs, and cultural outlets provided
within its borders that this program can reduce or
arrest the high mobility of the American people. The
solution to many of these problems requires far wider
involvement than just those local forces concerned
with a Model Cities area. Regional planning may be
needed while the continued input of state and federal
resources will have to be increased to solve them at
this higher level of planning. The first seeds for
this type of regional or metropolitan planning have
already been sown in the same Model Cities Act.

However, the feasibility of such comprehensive
planning across the political lines of many municipalities and autonomous functions of the numerous
authorities such as water, pollution, or transportation would be even more difficult to accomplish than

planning within the narrower geographic boundaries
envisioned in the Model Cities neighborhoods. Thus,
the success of the Model Cities program in meeting
many of the solutions of the poor would have to be
demonstrated first before real attention can be paid
to the metropolitan planning many visualize as being
the only way to solve the problems inherent in the
poverty areas. This rationale merely reinforces the
importance of the Model Cities program and its need
to be successful in meeting some of its stated objectives.

CHAPTER **2** THE MODEL CITY CONCEPT

THE URBAN CRISIS AND CHANGING
EXPECTATIONS

Although the reality of our urban problem needs
no proof, we would maintain that a critical component of the so-called urban problem is the result of
changing views of what society is about and the responsibility that must be borne for the individual
by the society. In our opinion, the fact of these
changed perceptions of an acceptable social order is
the first problem with which we must deal. As a
society, we must arrive at a workable statement of
our expectations of our social institutions and what
these changed expectations mean by way of active demands for social, educational, political, and economic progress. Similarly, we must arrive at a workable
statement of society's responsibility in supplying
the resources needed to satisfy these demands. In
other words, for our time and place, we must learn
to know what an acceptable social system is, and why
this system is acceptable to us. Having done this,
we may then be able to begin the laborious task of
gathering the knowledge needed for the creation of
those new social mechanisms and instruments that may
more fully satisfy these changed needs. Thus, it may
be necessary to back away momentarily from the crush
of our urban crisis in order to better understand the
root causes of this crisis. Once we have gained this
perspective, we may then be able to more intelligently attack an extremely comprehensive and pervasive
social problem.

This emphasis on changing expectations is not,
of course, meant to provide the excuse for denying
or glossing over the realities of our urban crisis.
The specter of poverty, discrimination, and bias are

still with us. Even though its incidence is considerably less than in 1945, and even though there are
legal impediments to its existence, discrimination
and bias are still very much a part of our everyday
life. Although progress has been made, it is a slow
and painful progress especially to those peoples and
groups who have either been left behind by this progress, or have just found out about its existence.
It is because of the visibility of this progress,
however, that the expectations and aspirations of our
urban poor have changed. Until the changed expectations and aspirations of our urban poor have been
converted into relevant actions by the powerholders
and the decision-makers, we will have urban unrest,
sometimes in active revolt, sometimes in a quiescent
state. But, the threat will remain with us until such
time as our expectations of our society and the realities of this society are more complementary than they
are at the present time.

THE REALITIES OF PLANNING

    Because of the reality of an active revolt, it is
obvious that change is essential--political change,
institutional change, and social change--and that
mechanisms for change must be developed and brought
into active operation. However, there is no guarantee that anyone really knows the direction, the scope,
or the content that this change should assume. The
lack of knowledge is manifest. First, there are few
people, even those in our power structure, who have
a sufficiently comprehensive view of the workings of
our society to provide either the planner or those
seeking change with an adequate description or model
of our political, economic, and social systems.
Second, those people seeking change do not now have
any ready prescription for an improved society that
is not, in general, a call for more of certain goods
and certain services to the neglect of others. Although the academic and intellectual community talks
about the realities of a "systems analysis," little
is really known of this technique and its applications to social problems. It is obvious that our social system has evolved in response to random pressures

and random possibilities, many of which are inconsistent, if not incompatible, with one another. There
is no guarantee that any revolutionary manipulation
of these variables will in fact produce a better social system than the existing one unless we assume
cynically that we live in the worst of all possible
worlds. Even the bloodiest of pessimists deny this!
Nonetheless, directed change is essential and, if
there is to be directed change, someone or some organization must take the responsibility for the planning that will eventually lead to a bevy of relevant
programs, structures, and tasks. But, the minute one
talks in terms of planning, a new problem appears.
First, no one is really certain about the nature and
content of the systemic changes that we wish to create. Second, no one really knows what is truly involved in planning for a society that has until now
been unplanned. Let us amplify that statement before
going further.

For the better part of two hundred years, we in
the United States have lived in a sort of laissez-
faire economically oriented society. At the federal
level, planning typically followed a simplified input-
output type of analysis. If the quality of medical
care is to be improved, the federal approach until
recently was to infuse massive sums of money into the
perceived area of need. This flow of funds was then
expected to bring about a form of change beneficial
to all of society. The rate and direction of this
change was, however, non-directed, since the federal
government supplied only the funds with the actual
program implementation subject for the most part to
local priorities, abilities, and controls. Thus,
the federal planning activity was really an "anti-
planning" effort, i.e., no specific operating goals
for a program were set. Instead, it was assumed that
the flow of funds into an area of need would activate
the "unseen hand" of economic growth that we sanguine-
ly believe guides our economy. But, if this is planning, it is, at best, macro-planning. And if results
have been generated by this type of planning, they
have been macro-results! Not that this approach is
necessarily wrong! Certainly, it is in keeping with
our perception of limiting central authority, the

maximizing of local initiative and innovation, and
our perceived natural ethic of self-reliance.

But this type of planning fails in certain crucial respects. First, this system of planning, because of existing power blocks and pressure groups,
can create an unwanted and socially destructive mis-
allocation of resources in the affected area of our
society. Structural impediments can rearely be
solved by macro-planning techniques. For example,
one of the key causes of the rapid increase in medical costs these past few years has been the rapid increase in the amount of federal funds available for
medical research. By bidding scarce medically
trained professionals out of active patient-care
areas, various federal programs built an inflationary
fire under the cost structure of the medical industry. The supply of community-oriented physicians
was reduced at a time when the demand for their services was increasing rapidly.

Second, even if one of the purposes of the federal subsidy to medical research is to increase employment and wage scales in the medical care industry,
macro-planning lacks the mechanisms needed to guarantee that these wage increases will be evenly and
equitably distributed. Because they control the delivery system for medical services, the physician
group has profited most by the existence of federal
subsidies both for medical research and for medical
care.

Third, the primary emphasis in most macro-planning
efforts is on influencing the supply side of the equa-
tion. Funds are normally provided to the providers of
services, and not the consumer in most macro-planning
efforts. As noted earlier, funds were devoted to increased medical research at a time when the supply of
physicians for our society was extremely limited. The
net result of this increased emphasis on research was
to decrease the supply of patient-oriented physicians
at a time when the demand for their services, because
of increased societal expectations, had increased.
Practically none of the macro-planning funds were devoted to increasing the supply of essential personnel
in keeping with total systemic needs. This, however,

is to be expected. Professionalism is a growing
reality of American society. Because of this, an increase in the funds allocated to an area of activity
controlled by a professionally oriented group can be
expected to increase their normal desire to deter the
entry of others into their profession. The professional group may be especially successful in this activity if they control the educational system that
schools the future professional and if there are few
obvious substitutes for the product that they provide.
This criticism is, of course, not aimed solely at the
medical profession. The growing militancy of school
teachers, social workers, and a full range of professional and quasi-professional people attest to the
realities of the situation.

Fourth, the reliance of the macro-planners on
local initiative and innovation is suspect in light
of the lack of a formal and viable statement of national goals and objectives. Macro-planning is too
loose and too non-directive if a specific effect upon a specific delivery system is desired. More detailed planning is essential. But, if this detailed
planning is accomplished at the national level, it is
again suspect. According to our political ethic the
planning process should be controlled at the local
level. The federal government should provide only
the cash needed to stimulate the activity and the
broadest possible set of guidelines. The non-
directive rationale here is, of course, good, if we
mean reliance on local initiative. The rationale
fails, however, if the planning talent is not available at the local level and if the federal guidelines
are so broad as to allow for idiosyncratic behavior.
The evidence now available strongly suggests that our
stock of planners is small, their skills relatively
undeveloped, and their behavior more idiosyncratic
than would appear to be justified.

PLANNING, ADMINISTRATION, AND POLITICS

Despite our limited knowledge about the art of
planning, we are still in agreement on the need to
do something of substance to alleviate the critical
conditions that now exist in many of our older urban

areas. That this "something" may be the wrong thing
to do is now quite evident to many of the more astute
observers of our urban crisis. Most planning efforts
are plagued with unexpected secondary outcomes that
may destroy the value or validity of the original
program. Nonetheless, this risk must be taken because of the greater risk of doing nothing. For example, we have begun training a corps of "City Planners"--people whose main predilection is in the
reconstruction of the physical environment of the
city, its buildings, roads, and public conveniences.
Their response to the needs of an urban society is
a well-reasoned response to the overwhelming physical
decay that has blighted many large sections of our
older cities. Although the city planner intuitively
recognizes that the physical rehabilitation of a city
is not the sole or the ultimate solution to the
ultimate problem, he similarly recognizes that half
a loaf is better than none. Perhaps, he reasons,
new public housing will motivate its inhabitants toward an active desire for the "better things in life"
that is the rationale of our vast middle class. Perhaps better office buildings will convince the business community that an urban location is superior to
a suburban one. But perhaps not. Clearly, people
have needs for other than office buildings, new
housing, and new civic centers. This is something
that the city planner knows, and something that the
general public is just now beginning to realize. New
buildings, or at least the need for new buildings,
is a peculiarly American middle-class value. They
may not be important or of great utility to the urban
poor whose needs we are proposing to fulfill. They
are, of course, valuable to the local politician
searching for "visibility." They are similarly valuable to the national body politic and for much the
same reason; they are visible, their construction
provides useful though limited employment, and they
fulfill an obvious need in an obvious manner. That
the people who inhabit them oftentimes regard them
as high-rise jails is a matter for the sociologist
and not the city planner or the politician. That
the people who inhabit them may have more pressing
needs than new housing is just now beginning to become painfully obvious to those who follow urban
trends.

These other needs have begun to float to the
surface only in the past few years because it has
suddenly become evident that if old buildings must
be torn down to make room for new public housing
something must then be done to help those people who
are temporarily or permanently uprooted from their
normal social setting. This evident need has helped
to create the role of yet another planner: the social planner whose function is to provide counseling
and assistance to the person who is about to be uprooted. This counseling is to provide the uprooted
with a statement of rights created for him by the
non-voluntary move and, in most instances, some cash
to help soften the shock. All of these services are
to be supplied provided that the dispossessed agrees
to move and accept the preconditions for this move
dictated to him by the hard, goods-oriented city planner. In theory, although not always in fact, the
newly minted city planner and the newly minted social
planner are to work hand-in-hand in first destroying
and then re-creating a "community." Indeed, the pre-
ation of a "community" is the function of most social
planners; relocation activities are but one part of
this total function.

That these planners may not truly understand the
community--its people, attitudes, and its value
judgments--is incidental to the problem at hand. They
are either presumed to understand these perceptions,
or the need for understanding these perceptions is
presumed to be non-existent. Both assumptions are
fallacious. Although there is a growing body of literature on community organization, the development
of a "sense of community," and "community cohesiveness," most of this literature is presently geared
to the needs of the academician and not the activist.
From a pragmatic point of view, we do not yet know
enough about the ways in which a "sense of community"
can be created in a large unstructured group such as
the ghetto, or how this sense of community can be
used to motivate the community and the individual
within it to an acceptable form of self-improvement.
We do know that this sense of community is "good,"
"essential," "motivating," and a whole host of other
adjectives whose intrinsic value we semantically accept. But, we do not know how to create a sense of

community, improve upon it, or use it as a vital tool
in creating a better society for all of us. The fact
is, we may not even understand how it affects our own
lives.*

     Part of our lack of understanding of this vital
phenomenon is an outgrowth of our social and political system. Local governments historically have
placed an emphasis upon maintaining and preserving
the perceived status quo by proposing to deliver to
their constituents what we have come to regard as a
neutral bag of services. The status quo has been
perpetuated, for example, by the enactment of restric-
tive zoning laws over protective construction codes,
and similar legislation. In general, the laws are
designed to protect what is--as opposed to stimulating
what should be. Admittedly, the laws and ordinances
were written and enacted at a time when the city was
regarded ecologically as a stable, non-dynamic factor.
These laws and ordinances were also enacted at a time
when the intellectual and political emphasis in our
society was upon descriptive, as opposed to normative,
concepts. For their time and in the context of their
time, they were good laws. But, the times have
clearly changed.

     Similarly, most local governments still continue
to deliver to their constituency this neutral bag of
services: garbage collection, tax collection, street
cleaning, and other housekeeping services that are
essential to the social order but add little to the

_____ _____

     *This paragraph created dissension in the authors'
ranks because of the existence of a growing body of
social welfare literature dealing with community organization. The point at issue is neither the existence of the literature, nor the ability to work
successfully with these constructs with very small
groups. Rather the point at issue is our ability to
apply this body of knowledge to large groups of people
such as exist in most Model Cities areas. Given the
present state of the arts of the social sciences, in-
ducing the derived effects in large population groups
is virtually impossible.

quality of life of the typical middle-class American.
Conversely, we must admit that these services--if
only because of their absence--represent quality of
life to the urban poor, who either do not receive
them or receive them in ineffectual amounts. The
point at issue, however, is not the services that
are provided, but rather the philosophic and administrative basis upon which these services have come
to be provided. In general, they are caretaker services delivered in an uncoordinated, poorly conceived
manner. What are the objectives of a city? What
functions should it perform in fulfilling their statement of goals? Caretaker services, or the quality of
life? Even our educational system, the one vital so-
cializing tool controlled and administered by our local governments, has either been neutralized or, in
the case of many core cities, been made negative in
the name of a false concept of political and social
equality: Every child in the community is to receive
the same form of education irrespective of his needs
or his aspirations. In many instances, this egali-
tarian premise has created a system that profoundly
perpetuates inequalities. Given our notion of the
political process, and the biases and the prejudices
with which we surround this process, people (and especially children) have been discriminated against
in the name of a true democracy.

Correcting these inequalities, however, can pose
a grave threat to those democratic processes to which
we are all committed. Any normative concept of a
social system--because it is a statement of what
should be--rests upon a series of value judgments.
The question of whose value judgments we are to accept then becomes a critical issue. How are we to
know whose prescription of what our society should
be is appropriate for all of us or even a majority
of us? How are we to know if it represents an improvement over what we now have? Thus, the political
process, particularly at the local level, is caught
between two pressures: the need to create a better
society and the need to avoid too rigorous and too
defined a statement of what our social and political
values should be. The rationale for the federal government's reliance on macro-planning thus becomes

self-evident. To the extent that we all propose to
believe in a self-adjusting economy, and to the extent this self-adjusting, price-oriented economy real
ly provides for the needs of our society, then it is
the function of the federal government to provide
funds for this economy and presume that society will,
through economic measures, make those adjustments and
adaptations that are most consistent with the demands
of the majority of our citizens. Our present system
is based on the notion that it is better to sacrifice
economic efficiency than individual autonomy or personal freedom.* Although there is a large segment of
our population that is unable to attain this autonomy
and freedom for themselves, the hope is that an ex-
panding economy will gradually grant them more contro
over their lives than they presently have.

From an economic point of view, macro-planning
treats money as if it were a pool of water. It spread
it around and hopes that it will cover both the low
and the high points of the problem area. By avoiding
a direct confrontation with the problem, one that is
usually structural in scope, macro-planning avoids
the necessity for detailed area or group specific
guidelines. In doing so, it tends to place more emphasis on individual freedom of choice than on economic efficiency.

The rub comes when the funds are insufficient to
the task. Unwieldy or impractical compromises in operating procedures must then be made by those who

----

*A second possible point of dissent between the
authors. Both obviously believe in personal autonomy and freedom. One author would maintain that
macro-planning helps to preserve this freedom by not
narrowly restricting the social welfare activities
of the local government. The other author would
maintain that the lack of funds, or the manner in
which the funds are allocated, is, in itself, a re-
strictive measure which is destructive of individual
autonomy and freedom. Both opinions are correct but
only from their narrow points of view; the reality
of the situation is somewhere in between.

control, or are responsible for, the delivery system.
This is usually the local government since, for the
most part, state and federal governments are resource
allocators and not service providers. Because of
the nature of its fund flow, local government is
forced to preserve its fiscal integrity by sharply
limiting the personal freedom of choice it grants to
its consumer group. This is especially so with the
welfare recipient wherein the funds normally available to the recipient are adequate only to maintain
life but not to provide the individual with the motivation or ability to break out of the cycle of poverty in which he finds himself. Thus, at the federal
level, personal sanctity appears to be maintained at
the expense of economic efficiency. At the local
level, the opposite is true. The conflict between
federal and local reality is, of course, the heart
of the matter of the unfitted expectations of the
poor.

Apart from the more obvious political issues,
however, there are a number of practical and vital
planning issues that require clarification. Our experience in the development in New York of a Model
Cities program taught us quickly that planning as now
practiced is a "broad-brush" exercise, and that the
typical planner knows little or nothing of the vital
interfaces between planning and administration. Indeed, it now seems evident to us that the typical
planner regards administration as the antithesis, if
not the outright enemy, of planning.

This failure to reconcile the art of planning
with the art of administration has been the focal
point for a great many failures in the public sector.
The planner decides what must be done but fails, because of his limited background or because of his
strong commitment to a social action process, to determine the time and the resources needed to convert
a plan into an operating program. The need for staff,
the time that it takes to recruit this staff, the
administrative process needed to weld this staff into
an effective working unit, and the initial need to
structure a feed-back mechanism into the administrative process are tasks that get neglected or forgotten

in the planning process. In many instances, the
failure to recognize the need for an administrative
process is due to the planner's lack of experience.
In other instances, it reflects his own professional
background wherein a detailed knowledge of management practices and procedures is not regarded as essential to the kit of tools provided to a planner.
Last, there is a group of planners--and especially
the social planners--whose prime motivation for their
activities is ethical and moral: the need to do
something "good" for society. This group regards
administration as a bureaucratic process to be avoided or even harassed on the assumption that bureaucracy is opposed to "progress."

Regardless of the cause, however, this lack of
concern for the administrative process is a root
cause of the failure of many planning efforts. The
planner forgets that program implementation is a management process that requires the development and the
implementation of an organizational structure. The
planner forgets that this organizational structure
has needs of its own: properly experienced administrators who can bring a program to life, a feed-back
mechanism that evaluates program inputs and outputs,
and the similar managerial considerations. Inherent-
ly, the organization is as much a part of the planning process as is the actual plan itself. Unlike
the planning group the operating organization must
deal daily with the need for hierarchical or bureaucratic structures and conflict. Similarly, it must
deal daily with the realities of the political and
social structure. When the planning process calls
for attitudinal or behavioral changes, the function
of administration is to lay the groundwork for these
attitudinal or behavioral changes. The failures of
the planning group to circumspectly adapt to the social and political realities that surround them will
become evident all too quickly. Even social progress
requires a knowledge of the art of compromise.

In addition, the planning process invariably cuts
across a multitude of governmental activities and
jurisdictions. Urban redevelopment, for example, gets
involved in questions of zoning, code enforcement,

income maintenance, and relocation expenses. Even in
a small city, two, three, even five or six agencies
may need to get involved as an ad hoc coordinating
group whose purpose is to facilitate the implementation of a desired project. The need for this group,
and its own program and administration, is often neglected by the planner whose primary focus is usually his own group or department. In addition, the
political orientation or necessities of each of the
participating departments is often neglected or played
down by the planner despite the fact that these political orientations may prove to be permanent impediments to constructive action. Each of the individual
departments has its own legal needs and requirements
which must, in the absence of legislative change, be
fulfilled. Any lack of adherence to previously established regulations may expose the departmental administration to serious legal charges and punishments.
The fractionated nature of the responsibility assigned to many municipal departments is an unfortunate
legacy of the late 1800's when our society, because
of its lack of faith in the political system, introduced legislation that severely limited the exercise
of certain types of political power. Many of these
laws were suited to the late 1800's when population
density, the intensity of poverty and personal deprivation, and societal patterns were radically different from what they are at present. Unfortunately,
many of these laws remain on the books, making the
tasks of interdepartmental planning, coordination,
and implementation more of a myth than a reality.
The Model Cities legislation is a federal attempt to
search for a way around these various obstacles by
the creation of a super-agency that can deal with a
specific portion of the city in a completely coordinated manner. The success of the program is vital
to a much-needed reassessment of the goals and functions of urban government. Unfortunately, the Model
Cities program has not yet been around long enough
to have had a meaningful impact on restatements of
urban goals and functions. Nonetheless, we firmly
believe that the lessons we learned in developing a
Model Cities program for New York City are applicable
and relevant to the crucial environmental and societal problems now faced by many of our core cities.

NEW YORK CITY

From an organizational point of view, New York
City was ideally suited for the development of a
Model Cities program. During 1966 and 1967, Mayor
John V. Lindsay created twelve super-agencies by linking together under a common authority or administration a number of previously autonomous agencies or
bureaus. Among the twelve super-agencies so created
was the Housing and Development Authority (HDA), the
super-agency for a number of smaller agencies previously responsible for housing, urban renewal, code
enforcement, and similar municipal services. The
Human Resources Agency (HRA) was similarly created to
coordinate and control the activities of the Department of Social Services, the city's welfare department; the Community Development Agency; the city's
anti-poverty program; and the Manpower Career and
Development Agency, the city's manpower training
agency. Representatives of two super-agencies, HDA
and HRA, were subsequently appointed to a newly
formed Model Cities Committee which included, in addition to the HDA and HRA representation, representatives from the mayor's office, the City Planning
Commission, the Housing Authority, the Bureau of the
Budget, and the Council against Poverty. This Model
Cities Committee was to advise in the development of
a Model Cities program. A specific Model Cities
planning effort was mounted shortly thereafter within the HRA even though the Model Cities appropriation
had not yet been voted out of Congress. The mayor
was reasonably certain that the legislation would
become law, as it did, and that the city would receive both planning and demonstration funds. He was
also convinced of the vital need, irrespective of
federal funding, for a Model Cities program that emphasized the coordination of existing human resource
activities.

Shortly after the creation within the HRA of the
post of Model Cities Coordinator and the mounting of
an initial planning phase concerned solely with planning for the human resources component of the Model
Cities program, a number of problems became evident
to those of us working on the plan:

(1) The proposed Model Cities legislation was
extremely loose and non-specific. An agency to be
called the City Demonstration Agency was to be created within the core city to deal, as best it could,
with the manifest problems of the ghetto. No definition of the scope or the content of these problems
existed. The new Model Cities agency was to define
the problems with which it wanted to deal. Among
other outcomes, this lack of specificity created the
atmosphere for argument and confusion amongst the
six key agencies that were to be involved in the total process. Each agency wanted to do only what it
knew best. This lack of specificity in problem definition helped to create an atmosphere of confusion
in which each agency pushed for its own definition
of the problem, with a minimum of emphasis on coordination.

(2) Instead of being limited to a specific functional area, this new coordinating agency was to deal
with the full range of social problems: education,
health, housing, unemployment, economic development,
and so forth. However, no real data on the scope or
the content of these problems existed to which the
Model Cities program could refer. This then meant
that the planning process would be further delayed
while essential data was collected and analyzed. Making the planning process even more complex was the
lack of trained data-collection and analysis personnel.

(3) The City Demonstration Agency itself was, at
least in its initial phase, required to develop its
own organizational structure. Because of its desire
to have the cities deal innovatively with their own
problems, Washington intentionally avoided mandating
any specific organizational structure. While providing the cities with the maximum degree of operating freedom, this lack of structure also placed
them in a most difficult position. Value judgments
on needs had to be made. In addition, decisions on
the priorities of these needs and the techniques to
be used in fulfilling these needs had to be made.
Given the lack of knowledge about the true nature and
full scope of these needs, the task of urban planning
becomes difficult if not impossible.

It soon become evident to those of us working in
New York City that a conceptual and administrative
framework for dealing with human resource problems
was essential. Without this framework, we could
travel around in circles never knowing our starting
or our end points. Without this framework, the Model
Cities program would end up in the same "bag" that
other program had: a series of disjointed programs
that only paid lip service to the real need of the
poor for a coordinated social services delivery system. Because of the question of value judgments, it
was also obvious to us that the Model Cities program
might not answer the needs of the poor but only the
limited perception of these needs held by the planner. For these reasons, we believed that there was
a need to establish philosophic and administrative
groundrules to which we could refer during the planning process.

In retrospect, we now feel that establishing
philosophic and administrative rules is a critical
element in all planning processes. These rules need
not be complex or sophisticated. Simple benchmarks
are adequate even for the Model Cities legislation
which calls for the creation of a better society
through institutional change. This, too, is critical
to an understanding of the legislation and the program that we attempted to create in fulfilling the
legislative mandate.

                THE QUESTION OF VALUE JUDGMENTS

The act of improving society involves an analysis
and a subsequent manipulation of many of the critical
value judgments around which that society is structured. In attempting to plan a Model Cities program,
we recognized that it would be impossible to meaningfully explicate these judgments in a manner concise and precise enough to be used as operational
objectives. Further, we did not believe then and we
do not believe now that a planning agency has the
right to tinker with these value judgments; changing
value judgments is the province of the courts, the
legislature, and, ultimately, the people. Any

planning process must recognize and be influenced by
these value judgments; it should not create them.
We suspect that this particular statement will be
met with a significant amount of criticism from those
of the planning profession who believe that their
mandate requires them to change value judgments. We
do not concur. Tinkering with society is tinkering
with the value judgments that have helped to create
that society. Planners tinker with society--indeed
that is their responsibility--and they must get involved in influencing these critical value judgments.
But the planner is normally a low-level person; he
represents a political group, may even be a part of
it but he is not normally the formal leader of the
group. Because of this he must be willing to consciously realize that an appropriately constituted
political body has the ultimate responsibility for
his acts. This body must be able (and be allowed)
to guide and control the activities of the planner.
This does not happen too often in the real world.
First, Americans have a unique fear of planning. For
reasons which are not completely clear, Americans do
not like to make explicit the value judgments on
which their society is built. Second, most administrators appear to lack a concrete knowledge of the
planning process and thus treat the whole notion of
planning in an almost offhand manner. As an academic
discipline, planning is normally taught within the
context of social action. Knowledge of the planning
process is not generally linked to a knowledge of the
management sciences despite the vast body of knowledge that the management sciences possess on the
linkages between administration and planning. The
failure to link these two disciplines is at the hub
of many planning failures. The plan exists; the administrative structure to bring it into reality does
not.

    Despite all of this, however, planning must be
done. And to make it relevant to the needs of the
people it proposes to serve, planning must be constrained by an explicit statement and understanding
of existing societal values. Without an awareness
of these values, and the effect of these values on a
programmatic structure, planning may lead to the

implementation of action tools that create a whole
new value structure that is either unacceptable to
society as a whole or unacceptable to the proposed
recipients. Many of the critical problems now facing
us are the outcomes of prior planning efforts that
failed to systematically assess the long-term structural and philosophic effect upon society of a specific plan of action. Primary effects of proposed
actions are easily perceived. It is the unexpected
secondary effect, however, that distorts the original
concept or goal of the planning group. In our Model
Cities planning we wanted to avoid this shortcoming
if it was humanly possible to do so. Because of this,
we gradually evolved a number of statements of understanding as guides for our planning efforts. Some
of these guidelines were of an administrative nature.
Some represented a modicum of conceptual thinking.
In each case, we tried to be guided by the validity
of the guidelines and not their conceptual or administrative sophistication, since we were more concerned
with the product of the planning process than the process itself. Some of the key guidelines we developed
are as follows:

(1) The vast majority of Americans purchase the
greater part of their "social service" needs from
the private sector. This has been traditional in our
country and apparently representative of the desires
of the vast majority of Americans. We believe that
the poor--the target of the Model Cities program--
should have the same right, and that the primary responsibility of the Model Cities program is to evolve
a viable economic development and manpower training
program that will help them achieve the income which
will allow them to purchase from the private sector
those services that they desire. Until such time as
they are able to do this, however, the provision of
these services must remain the responsibility of the
local government.

(2) By themselves, economic development and manpower training programs will accomplish very little.
If unsupported by a complete range of traditional
social welfare services, manpower training or an economic development program will merely serve to skim

off the limited number of the poor who are normally
upwardly mobile while leaving behind an even harder
hard core. To avoid this, basic social services designed to deal with the non-economic "disabilities"
of the poor must be incorporated into a Model Cities
program. Further, the Model Cities program must be
prepared to "sell" these programs to its client
group. In other words, a Model Cities program must
be prepared to cope with the general lack of an effective demand for essential services that character-
izes the poor and to stimulate this demand by offering
services that the poor recognize as valid. The causes
for this lack of demand for vital social services are
many:

- The poor distrust the establishment; they
  don't trust the "product" provided them by
  the typical social welfare agency, or the
  conditions under which these services have
  heretofore been provided to them. Too often
  it has been a case of too little and too late.

- The poor do not even know of the existence
  of many of these services. Local governments
  generally do not advertise their products.

- They know little or nothing of the value to
  them of these services.

For these reasons, a community education process
that may develop an essential "sense of community"
amongst the poor is essential. In other words, let
people perceive for themselves that the product of
an anti-poverty program is helpful and of value to
them, and encourage them to take advantage of the
provided services.

(3) Thus, the Model Cities program must recognize
the validity of the economic concept of consumer
sovereignty and choice. By helping to provide the
poor with the necessary access to jobs and income it
should provide them with this request. During this
process, furthermore, the Model Cities program should
provide them with a broad range of social services
that helps them become more meaningfully integrated

in the society that exists around them. Or at least
able to deal better with this society! By participating in the planning process, the poor should also
be given the right to influence the range of services
to be made available to them. In addition, they should
have the ability to pick and choose among the services
that they specifically want. Social services cannot
be impressed upon an unwilling audience. In business
language--the programmatic structure of Model Cities
is a product, and the poor are the market for these
services. But they must be convinced of the value of
these services, and not by the providers of these
services whom they tend to distrust, but rather by
their peers who have fully participated in, and fully
understand, the planning process. In this context,
the participation of the poor can be regarded as a
highly sophisticated marketing strategy. Although
this may appear to be too philistine a statement--it
sounds as if manipulation is being suggested--the
opposite is true in the more affluent sectors of our
society. The P.T.A., the League of Women Voters, and
membership on a hospital or church board are marketing devices used to provide support and sanction for
an organization.

   (4) The Model Cities program structure must be
two-edged. It must concern itself with the creation
in the core city of a better community, but it must
do so in a way that gives the poor the ability to improve their lot so that they can desert the ghetto _if
they so desire_. We later termed this notion the
"Transmission Belt Concept"--and held to this view
despite the statement of many Negro leaders about
their desire for a separate but equal society. First
of all, we failed to perceive the realities or the
equity of separate but equal black communities. We
firmly believe that all people must have the right to
live where they desire. To some extent, we are saying
that the Negro leader speaks for only a segment of
black society. We assume that there are many blacks
who prefer to speak for themselves. In programmatic
terms, this means that the Model Cities administration
must be prepared to provide rehabilitative services
for those who choose to remain in the ghetto, and developmental service for those who wish to leave. The

Model Cities program is to bring about institutional
change by linking together existing organizations and
structures in a way that will improve the quality and
the effectiveness of the social services delivered to
the consumer. Although we visualize and understand
the eventual need for the creation of new institutions
and programs, we basically believe that the first order of business of a Model Cities program is to coordinate innovatively and imaginatively existing
community resources. Based upon our review of existing New York City programs, we believe that there is
a vital need for many existing organizations to assess
the validity of the services that they now provide
their client groups. Once again, based upon an assessment of the output of various social service agencies, we believe these agencies are no longer relevant
to the needs of the population that they propose to
serve, and that this irrelevance is an underlying
factor in creating the citizen dissatisfaction that
is now endemic in our society.

(5) Last, we agreed on the use of a construct that
we labeled the "Life Cycle Hypothesis." This hypothesis was no more than an attempt to develop an admin-
istratively viable description of societal needs as a
function of the age of the individual. This concept
proved to be extremely helpful to us in a number of
ways, and will be discussed at greater length in
Chapter 3. For example, by using this hypothesis we
were able to synthesize a full range of societal needs
and from this the programmatic needs of an individual
over the full span of his lifetime. The explication
of this relationship led us first to the notion of a
"basic" and a "support" program and from there to some
basic cost-benefit techniques, which we developed
around generally accepted economic concepts of fixed
and variable costs.

In addition, using the matrix that we developed
for expressing in simple terms the relationships inherent in a life cycle hypothesis, we were able to
recognize the shortcomings of a program-oriented welfare system. Individual programs do not, for the
most part, do a complete job for the client. Individual programs need reinforcement from supplementary

programs delivered within the context of a total need.
Although the "output" of a Model Cities effort is a
series of projects or programs, to be effective a
Model Cities program must, in the final analysis, be
a process. The use of a life cycle hypothesis pointed
this out and helped to keep us on target in our planning effort.

Last, and perhaps most critical of all, the use
of a life cycle hypothesis helps to expose the programmatic deficiencies with which any ostensibly comprehensive program must live. Resources are scarce.
Effective social welfare programs are expensive. It
is impossible for one program, even one as potentially comprehensive as the Model Cities program, to fulfill the lifetime needs of an individual or a group
of individuals. The use of a life cycle hypothesis
and a matrix in explanation of this concept pinpoints
the limitations of any proposed program and its administrative structure. In our case, it led us to
the real need for linking public and private sector
resources. Because of the great cost of most individually oriented social service programs, private-sector
support of the Model Cities program is completely essential.

An analysis of the matrix similarly alerted us
to the need for a strong administrative mechanism
capable of efficiently coordinating either existing
or proposed programs. Last, the use of the hypothesis
made the need for an evaluation process quite clear.

These statements of understanding are not profound, nor are they meant to be. We did not discover
the wheels. What we attempted to work out--and we
believe we succeeded--was a communications device for
explicating our work and the premises upon which it
is built. Because of this, we were able later to
recognize directly the cause of certain administrative
and planning successes and failures. Also, the life
cycle hypothesis helped us to avoid the box of re-
strictive value judgments. We were able to understand
if only in a limited way, the value judgments that we
either made or had forced upon us. Because of this,
our planning effort was not conducted in a conceptual

vacuum. A fuller discussion of some of these statements of understanding and their relationship to the
planning process follows.

CHAPTER **3** THE NEW YORK MODEL
CITIES PROGRAM

BACKGROUND

The goals for the New York Model Cities program
were clearly defined in its initial application to
HUD for a planning grant. These goals called for
concerted action in the areas of:

(1) Environmental improvement;
(2) Social services;
(3) Early childhood education;
(4) Manpower; and
(5) The participation of the poor in the
planning process.

The general nature of the statement of these
goals is, of course, to be expected. By general con-
census, this broad statement of goals and objectives
is sufficient for grant application and policy purposes. The difficulty for the planner comes in the
conversion of these goals into specific operating
programs that efficiently deliver valid services to
the proposed client group. In New York City, the
primary responsibility for this conversion process
was assigned to a Model Cities Office, which was part
of the office of the Mayor.

In some respects, the appointment by HRA of a
Model Cities Coordinator for social planning was a
needless redundancy. As a super-agency, the HRA was
already responsible for coordinating and amalgamating
the City of New York's various human resource programs.
The New York anti-poverty program, its welfare function
and its manpower training activities were the direct
responsibility of the HRA. Because of this, the HRA

with its 1967 budget of $1.1 billion was, in and of itself, a Model Cities program. If properly coordinated, the HRA's existing program structure could be capable of delivering, to a substantial portion of the poor of New York City, those vital services called for in a Model Cities program. The HRA may still do so in the future as it learns more about the planning process.

The HRA, however, was involved at the time of the Model Cities planning in an internal struggle of its own. First, the four participating agencies which constituted the HRA in 1967 and 1968 had organizational structures and loyalties of their own. In the final analysis these three agencies were not willing to work together in the lock-step fashion called for by a Model Cities program. Second, the Youth Service Board, the Community Development Agency, which is the community action program component of the HRA, and the Manpower Career and Development Agency are primarily planning and resource-allocating bodies. They have little internal delivery systems capabilities of their own, and reach the community only through the so-called "delegate or contract agency"--a pre-existing social services agency that looks to the basic agency for funds. For reasons to be discussed later, the HRA failed to objectively analyze the program structure of these pre-existing agencies. It had little knowledge of the actual services that they proposed to deliver, and their ability to deliver the services. As a result of this, the HRA was not genuinely knowledgeable about the content, the quality, or the quantity of services being delivered to the deprived of New York City, even though they were in the position of funding these agencies. Further, the HRA had only the vaguest perception of the constituencies served by these agencies, and how the activities of the various agencies might best be coordinated if coordination were desired.

The reasons for the failure of the HRA to develop a working knowledge of its own programmatic structure are significant:

(1) The HRA was itself a new organization. It was never given the time by the community at large to

work out its own organizational structure and relationships. Because of political and community pressure, it was forced into "visible" actions long before
it had developed its own philosophy, mode of operation
and personality. Like many another anti-poverty program, it had been thrown too soon into the limelight.
The focus on its projected activities was taken by the
poor as a promise of immediate action. When this immediate action failed to materialize, both the community and the HRA became disillusioned.

(2) The task that the HRA publicly proposed to
take on was far too great a burden for any new agency.
A preliminary analysis of New York City reveals, for
example, that there are more than 2,000,000 poverty-
level people in the City. The notion of delivering
a coordinated and complete package of services to
2,000,000 people is staggering. The resources needed
for such a program are beyond the imagination of the
typical planner and beyond the present financial and
organizational ability of any governmental unit. At
best, an organization like the HRA can expect to deliver only a limited range of services and to a limited number of people. But the anti-poverty program
and the Model Cities program both represent themselves
as dealing with the entirety of the problem for the
entirety of their target population. The critical
problem of unanswerable aspiration levels is thus
created.

(3) Organizationally, at least through the early
part of 1968, the HRA did not know what direction to
take except in a general sort of way. It lacked a
vitally needed information system capable of monitor-
ing its own activities, to say nothing of the activities of its delegate agencies. One of the first
actions taken by the newly created HRA Model Cities
Office was to review the budget and organizational
relationships established by the HRA. In addition,
a rather superficial survey was made of the HRA delegate agencies in order to gain some first-hand knowledge of their activities. This review determined,
for example, that the HRA had not spent its full budget for things such as the Headstart program and manpower training programs. Funds had been allocated for

these various programs but nothing further had happened. No one in formal positions of authority in
the agency was aware of this simple fact. Because
the key people in the agency were so beset with critical political problems, they were unable to pay sufficient attention to critical administrative details.
In committing itself overwhelmingly to the notion of
social action, the HRA failed to develop the administrative structure it needed to deliver those services that it had promised to deliver. The HRA was
caught up in the web of its own aspirations, a situation that culminated in widespread administrative
laxity. This laxity, as reported in the New York
Times in January, 1969, resulted in the embezzlement
from HRA of large sums of money.

    In all fairness, however, no one should have ex-
pected the HRA to do all of those things to which it
had committed itself. First of all, the organization
was hastily assembled in late 1966. People were at-
tracted away from a number of key local, federal and
state agencies and thrown together in a wholly unstructured environment. Although efforts were made
to develop an administrative structure, these efforts
received little support from the top-level HRA people
who were far too busy putting out political fires.
Indeed, the HRA itself seemed to draw fire from those
city agencies whose support it had a right to expect.
The Model Cities effort, which is the subject of this
book, was mounted shortly after the creation of the
HRA, even though the HRA had not yet worked out the
realities of its own programmatic structure. No organization as new as this should have been expected
to control more than $1.1 billion in social welfare
programs in so short a period of time. Unfortunately,
HRA's failure to assess its own capabilities and to
set realistic timetables for performance was the root
cause of the defection in late 1967 and early 1968 of
many of its key planners and administrators. In final analysis of the charismatic force that helped to
create the HRA was not capable of holding it together.

    If nothing else, the failure of the HRA to become
fully operational within three years says something   .
vital about the art of planning, the political process

in which planning is involved, and the need for representatives of the planning group to be able to make clear and concise statements on the gestation period needed to give life to a programmatic structure. All of these lessons must be learned if the art of planning is ever to become refined enough to produce the end results desired by our society. Given our lack of knowledge about broad-scale social planning, failures must be expected and tolerated. The process of planning is difficult. Until a great deal is learned through trial and error about this process, we will not be able to convert this planning process into a planning product.

In order to be really understood, the Model Cities program must be viewed presently as a stimulus to planning. To be of value to the nation, the first output of the Model Cities program must be some well-defined and documented knowledge about the planning process, particularly the technique for gaining true inter-organizational cooperation. The second output must be a technique for meaningfully relating community needs to community resources since the deficiency between needs and resources is the first order of business of any general planning process. This planning process should, in turn, lead to a statement of objectives which, in turn, form the basis for programmatic planning. Program planning then becomes a secular process of specific service to a specific group of consumers. The delivery system is the administrative process which completes the program planning phase. The results of this secular planning process, however, must be fed back into an on-going general planning process so that this planning process can be modified or altered as the need becomes evident. But all of this requires time: time to develop a planning group that can work together; time to develop the plans from which programs flow; and time in which to implement programs. Thus, in our opinion, the first function of the Model Cities program should be to develop the planning and administrative experience that allows an organization to deal with complex social problems. The second function must be to develop an accurate awareness of the time needed to plan and to implement effective program structures. Until

this learning process has been completed, we can expect only a limited amount of social progress to be
produced by the Model Cities or related welfare programs.

ADMINISTRATIVE TOOLS AND THE PLANNING PROCESS

We arrived at the notion of the life cycle hypothesis plus a number of other administrative tools
pretty much by accident. Because we perceived that
the "coordination of existing resources" would be the
hub of the Model Cities process, we began an early
investigation of the organizational and programmatic
structure of the HRA. The purpose of this investigation was to develop an understanding of existing HRA
programs, their goals and objectives, the target
groups that they served or proposed to serve, and the
functions that they performed in doing all of this.
By doing this, we hoped to uncover programmatic deficiencies that might form the initial basis for a supplementary Model Cities effort. We also hoped to be
able to develop a more clear-cut notion on the need
for coordination and the way in which this coordination might be achieved. Last, we hoped to uncover
some ideas that might lead to concepts about the rationalization of program structures that might in
turn provide us with some clues for dealing with cost-
benefit problems.

In the process of inventorying and assessing
HRA's programs, we collected a substantial amount of
data which we recognized would be useless to us unless
we were able to place this data into a workable framework. This attempt at classification led us to the
life cycle hypothesis, which is no more than a matrix
which relates the basic personal and communal needs
of a person to a specific phase of his life, and then
relates these two factors to a programmatic or organizational structure that should be capable of providing an answer to these age-related needs.

The hypothesis starts out with two lists. One
list contains ten basic personal and community needs.
The second list contains a series of age groupings.

TABLE 1

Stages in the Life Cycle

Basic Needs	0-5	6-18	19-22	23-50	51-65	65 and over
Medical Care	Preventative, pediatrician	Preventative, pediatrician, G.P., specialists	Preventative, G.P., specialists	Preventative, G.P., specialists	Preventative, rehabilitative specialists	Rehabilitative specialists
Education	Pre-school, Head Start, nursery, kindergarten	Public and private basic education, vocational training, "special education"	Advanced education, college,. OJT, vocational training	Advanced education, professional and graduate, re-training, adult basic education, vocational training	Maintenance education, low-skill training, information about retirement benefits	Information about retirement benefits
Shelter	1-2 bedrooms	2-4 or more bedrooms	1-2 bedrooms	2-4 or more bedrooms	1-2 bedrooms	1-2 bedrooms
Job Opportunities		Home tasks, part-time jobs for spending money	Beginning need for secure income, unskilled, OJT, temporary jobs, low-echelon rank	Income security, income increasing, semi-skilled, skilled, technical, white collar and professional jobs, low-middle echelon rank	Income security, income stabilized, same but middle-high-echelon rank	Income security, public support, hobbies, part-time or temporary jobs

Recreation	Enclosed areas, structured or supervised play near the home	Organized athletics, large recreation areas, summer camps, YMCA	Recreation facilities (bowling, athletic clubs, amateur athletics)	Recreation facilities, entertainment or non-participant sports	Recreation facilities, entertainment, non-participant sports	Entertainment, non-participant sports
Community Activities	Church nursery school, playmates	Church Sunday school, youth organizations, clubs, YMCA	Church, politics, unions, community action, clubs	Church, politics, unions, business clubs, service and social clubs, community action	Same, more leadership status	Church, Golden Age clubs
Transportation	To medical centers, nurseries--walk	To schools, part-time jobs, entertainment--walk, bicycle, public transport, car	To jobs, schools, business section, recreation, entertainment areas, vacation--public and private transport, car	To jobs, business section, medical, entertainment and recreation, vacation--public and private transport, car	Same	To business district, medical centers--public and private transport
Business Services	Food, clothing, shelter	Food, clothing, shelter, recreation, car maintenance	Food, clothing, shelter, recreation, financial services, car maintenance	Same but more "luxury" items	Same, less quantity	Same, more services

(Continued)

71

TABLE 1 (Continued)

Basic Needs	0-5	6-18	19-22	23-50	51-65	65 and over
Cultural Activities	Creative toys, TV	Libraries, movies, museums, concerts, "Heritage" programs, TV, radio	Libraries, museums, movies, concerts, travel, TV, radio, theatre	Same	Same	Same
Social Services	Child guidance clinic, ADC grant	Pre-marital information, psychiatric help, vocational counseling	Pre- and post-marital aid, welfare, psychiatric help, vocational counseling, child care	Same	Welfare, psychiatric help	Social security, welfare

The needs we defined were:

    (1) Medical care
    (2) Education
    (3) Shelter
    (4) Work
    (5) Recreation
    (6) Community activities
    (7) Transportation
    (8) Business services
    (9) Cultural services
  (10) Special services

In much the same manner, we also defined specific age groupings. The following age classifications were defined:

    (1) Age 0-5 prekindergarten
    (2) Age 6-18 school years
    (3) Age 19-22 army, first job, or college
    (4) Age 23-50 work, raising a family
    (5) Age 51-65 work, freedom from children
    (6) Age 65+ retirement

Neither list is comprehensive nor completely correct pragmatically or conceptually, nor is it meant to be. Indeed, the lists are simply representative of a broad range of critical personal and community needs that must be dealt with in any comprehensive human resources program. Since the HRA was in the human resources business, we expected that we could relate any HRA program to at least one of the needs and one of the age groups listed above. In similar fashion, we also assumed that we could place any Model Cities program that might be developed during the planning process into some box on the matrix formed by relating these two lists.

It is possible, of course, to divide the age groups into other combinations, to subdivide them, or otherwise alter them for focus on a specific age or problem category. For example, the 6-18 category can be broken down into a 6-14 in-school and a 15-18 drop-out group. The rationale for creating a specific age group is obviously less important than is the process

of identifying personal or community needs as a function of the age of the individual.

As noted above, the two lists were linked into
the matrix shown in Table 1. We then completed the
matrix by placing it into age and need-related programs, facilities, or organizational structures that
could deal meaningfully with the age-related problems
that we had earlier specified. As the exhibit shows,
we did not search for sophistication or completeness
in the matrix. The mere creation of a taxonomy to
which we could refer when needed helped us to understand the planning process that we were undertaking.
This was all that we were looking for.

In our initial attempts at developing programs,
we found that we tended to cluster programs either
around well-defined age groups, or well-defined needs.
The notion of comprehensiveness, which is the essence
of the Model Cities program, slipped by us since we
soon found that we were unable to develop a comprehensive and potentially effective package of programs
or services unless we "solved" more than one problem
at a time. In other words, the poor suffer from a
multiplicity of disabilities and more than one disability must be solved simultaneously if there is to
be substantive progress in any one area. Thus, it
became evident that if a basic program or package of
services is developed to "cure" a specific disability,
it most likely will not succeed unless a package of
supporting programs is simultaneously developed to
guarantee the success of the basic program. This one
concept we found missing in most of the planning efforts that we reviewed as part of our Model Cities
responsibilities. More will be said of this later.

These facts of the planning process did not, of
course, immediately become obvious to us. The first
began to become evident when we attempted to gather
together data on existing HRA programs, the objectives
of these programs, the functions that were developed
to implement these objectives, and the resources
available for the defined task. Once this task was
underway, the need for a technique for relating the
content and the potential effect on the target population of these various programs became evident.

Although we could rationalize intuitively the planning process, and similarly arrive at some notion of program linkages, we were initially deterred from rationalizing a proposed programmatic structure until we defined a program as either "basic"--dealing directly with a defined disability--or "support"--responding to second level disabilities that deter the solution of the primary disability. For example, if we defined unemployment as the primary disability of "mothers, age 20-30, with children at home" and proposed a manpower training program to solve this problem, the basic program then became the manpower training process. The support program in this case becomes the day-care center which allows the mother to safely leave the home (the secondary disability) to prepare for work. Recourse to this technique, of course, underscores the complexity of any human resource program and the collateral or secondary costs not normally included in the planning of a basic program. Upon experimentation with these concepts, we found that classifying programs into a basic or support category simplified the cost-effectiveness analysis that should be performed on each proposed program. This led us quickly to the realization that a cost-effectiveness analysis is meaningless for most social welfare programs since their output is neither readily quantified nor visible. Nonetheless, these programs are essential "overhead" in any major welfare program. When this became evident, we turned to the industrial notion of fixed and variable costs as an explanation of the process with which we had been experimenting. To our surprise, the notion seemed to work both conceptually and programmatically. Thus, in experimenting with the development of a life cycle hypothesis, we ended up by talking in terms of basic and support programs, primary and secondary disabilities, and fixed and variable costs. We found these constructs an invaluable aid to the planning process. As the planning process became more articulate, we also found ourselves talking about "natural groupings," "the transmission belt concept," and the "freedom of choice." More will be said of these ideas later.

Conversely, the matrix that we developed helped to make evident the political game of "visibility" that can be played with any social welfare program.

There are some needs--a basic improvement in the public education system, for example--that take an extremely long time and a vast amount of money to
effect. Because of this, a program of this type usually lacks the support of a political group concerned
with visibility. Instead these power groups want in-
stant results to which they can point. The planner
must respond in this case immediately with highly
visible programs, such as Neighborhood Youth Corps
programs. Programs of this type are easy to mount,
require little professional background, and they
"push" money out to the population quickly and visibly
Because of this, they find ready political acceptance
although, as in the case of New York City, they may
create undesirable secondary effects such as an increase in the high school dropout rate. Internally,
because of the vast sums of money involved, they may
lead to the type of corruption uncovered in New York
in late 1968 and early 1969.

BASIC AND SUPPORT PROGRAMS

As noted earlier, our concern for the validity of
the life cycle hypothesis as a planning tool led us
to the development of a number of other planning tools
or constructs. The notion of basic and support programs was another such critical construct. This construct evolved after we began a review of the
operations and the cost factors involved in mounting
training programs. In order to understand this process, we carefully restricted the size and the characteristics of the population to be served by the program. Thus, we began to synthesize a manpower training
program for "unemployed males, ages 19-22, Negro or
Spanish-speaking Americans, who live in the ghetto."
We immediately recognized that one key reason for the
unemployment among this population was the basic lack
of work skills and work experience that is typical of
the ghetto-bound underemployed or unemployed. The
usual solution to this problem is to mount a skills
or manpower training program oriented almost solely
toward the development of technical skills.

In reviewing the statistics of some of these programs, however, it became evident that the rate of

success of many of these programs is minimal if success is measured by the number of persons with jobs
six months after the completion of the program.   Indeed, in one program of 1,000 persons, only 40 per
cent of the participants completed the program. The
reason for this low success rate, it soon became evident, is the fact that most participants in the program have a number of basic disabilities which are
not solved by a skills training program. For example,
there are a great number of mothers with children at
home who cannot remain with a program of this type if
there are no day-care nurseries for the care of their
pre-school children. In addition, most program participants lack basic educational skills. Because of
this, they are not able to keep up with the educational pace of the program and become understandably
disillusioned after two, four, or six months. Because of this, a basic job-skill training program
must be supplemented by a series of support programs
that are developed in coordination and in conjunction
with the basic program.

In structuring any program for this particular
target group, it is essential to think in terms of
a whole range of supplementary support programs; day-
care centers are not the only need.

Going one step further, it also means that specific funds must be allocated both for the basic program
and for the support programs. By segregating the inputs in this manner, one is then able to measure the
relative cost-effectiveness of each of the support
components and thus develop a mix of support programs
that appear to optimize the efficiency of the basic
program. This type of analysis is admittedly naive,
but it is a first step forward. For example, if a
skills training program without a day-care facility
for young mothers had existed previously, it then becomes reasonably easy to determine the marginal cost
of the day-care facility and the marginal benefit
provided by this facility as measured: by the larger
number of people who complete the program, and remain
gainfully employed. As noted earlier, the day-care
center is but one example of a support program that
can be developed in conjunction with a basic program.
Clearly, there are other support activities that are

needed, such as transportation services, remedial
education, health care, and so forth. If these services already exist in the community, linking them
to the basic program may involve no more than a minimal cost. If the support programs do not exist,
however, the start-up costs may be quite substantial
and produce little "evident" benefit for quite some-
time. This, however, brings us to the notion of fixed
and variable costs.

FIXED COSTS AND VARIABLE COSTS

In late 1967 and early 1968, the HRA consisted of
four key operating agencies:

(1) The Department of Social Services, form-
     erly the Welfare Department of the City
     of New York;

(2) The Youth Services Board, a previously
     autonomous agency that concentrated on
     neighborhood youth activities in specified
     low-income neighborhoods;

(3) The Community Development Agency, the
     anti-poverty and social action agency
     created under the aegis of the anti-
     poverty (OEO) program; and

(4) The Manpower Career and Development Agency,
     an outgrowth of Department of Labor pro-
     grams.

For analytical reasons, the almost $1 billion per
year allocated to the Department of Social Services
(DOSS) was kept separate from the HRA allocation of
approximately $110,000,000 per year. First, the
greater bulk of the DOSS's money is devoted to the
income maintenance programs typical of most welfare
agencies, and to the internal operations of the DOSS.
Second, the DOSS is so vast an agency--and has been
around for so long a period of time--that organizationally it resists the type of action oriented program structure called for in the HRA mandate. These

action oriented programs were to be provided by the
Community Development Agency (CDA), the Manpower
Career and Development Agency (MCDA), and the Youth
Services Board. For this reason, our goals and tasks
analysis of the HRA's activities, and the effect of
these activities on the target population, included
only the organizational and program structures of
these three agencies.

In 1967, and again in 1968, the projected combined
budget for these three agencies was approximately
$110,000,000. Approximately $65,000,000 of this sum
was to be spent by the CDA for packaged community action programs such as Head Start and health clinics.
The MCDA was allocated $35,000,000 primarily for man-
power and skills training programs.* Because of the
observed content, no deep or detailed analysis of the
components of the programs of both of these agencies
was needed to arrive at the conclusion that a cost-
benefit or even a cost-effectiveness analysis of the
CDA program structure as it then existed would be
relatively meaningless. Although we recognized that
social action programs do indeed have quantifiable
outputs, we similarly recognized that measuring and
quantifying these outputs in dollars and cents is nigh
unto impossible. Conversely, a cost-effectiveness or
cost-benefit analysis for a manpower training or work-
skills program can be a relatively straightforward
task provided that requisite data on inputs and outputs are recorded. This is not to imply that we intended to perform either a cost-benefit or cost-
effectiveness analysis on any of these programs, or
that we were capable of doing so. This was not the
task that had been assigned to us. Nonetheless, we
recognized the logic behind such an analysis, and regarded as essential our thinking through some of the
cost-benefit relationships that might be obtained by
various programmatic relationships. If nothing else,
this type of thought process provided us with a greater appreciation of the administrative complexity of

_____

*Because the Youth Services Board is the smallest
component of the HRA, it will not be included in this
discussion.

program implementation, and of the administrative
organization that would have to be invoked if meaningful cost-benefit or cost-effectiveness studies
were to be made.

Nonetheless, there was still the reality of a
$110,000,000 annual HRA budget. And there was the
reality of a 65:35 split. In theory, the 65:35 decision should have been arrived at rationally after
a great degree of analysis by the appropriate
decision-makers on the needs of the population and
the resources available for meeting these needs. In
practicality, we recognized that the decision on the
65:35 split was made intuitively. There would have
been little or no discussion of the economics or
cost-benefit structure of social welfare programs
during the decision-making process. Political realities, the availability of delegate agencies for
proposed tasks, the ability to synthesize new of different programs, the requests or claims of favored
people or institutions had all been taken into account in the coalition that constituted the decision-
making group. For better or for worse, the decision-
makers had arrived intuitively at a 65:35 funding
split; their intuition then ratified the rationality
of this split. We could, of course, accept this
split as rational or reject the notion of rationality. In the final analysis, we presumed rationality
in the decision-making process, but only because it
provided us with a needed description of the relative
importance and priority attached to various goals and
objectives. We could not, however, accept the 65:35
funding split as a normative statement of priorities
or programmatic relationship. And it was this normative statement that we believed we would eventually
need if ever we were to make a valid attempt at rationalizing the structure of any proposed Model Citie
program.

The more we looked at the CDA program structure,
however, the more evident it became that community
action programs are, in the final analysis, primarily
concerned with the acculturation and socialization
process. Head Start programs provide supplementary
education to the very young; they try to give the

Head Start student a helpful push into the earlier
years of the educational process by providing him
with a sense of confidence and awareness of group
behavior. Although the programs are also concerned
with the remediation process, they are nonetheless
supportive in the sense that their output, an enhanced
ability on the part of the individual to accommodate
himself to the world around him, is essentially an
acculturation and socialization process. In our
opinion, this is their critical long-term output.
This type of output cannot be measured in the short
term, nor should it be.

Similarly, health care programs are basic in that
they deliver specific services to specific people in
need of care. But they are also supportive in that
they are designed to help the individual to cope with
existing communal or personal deficiencies that destroy or otherwise inhibit his desire and ability to
attain social and economic advancement. Although one
can synthesize a short-term output for a neighborhood-
based health care program, we do not consider doing
so a valid exercise in the context of a long-term
Model Cities program. In our opinion, the true focus
of such a health care program is the long-term cor-
rection of basic and fundamental deficiencies in the
existing health care delivery system. Once again,
the output of this type of program should not in our
opinion be measured in anything but the long term.

Conversely, a skills or manpower training program
is a device for directly improving the economic condition of the individual. If there are mechanisms for
collecting the data, the benefit of this type of program can be validly measured in the short term, even
though short-term results if extrapolated to the long
term may overstate the level of benefits provided by
the program. The critical point at issue here is that
the manpower program, as an anti-poverty program or a
Model Cities device, is self-justifying in that it
automatically and directly raises the successful participant's income above the poverty level. In the
final analysis, this is the "name of the game" for any
anti-poverty or Model Cities program. The community
action program, however, neither attacks directly the

problem of poverty nor does it attempt to do so. Instead, this type of program is designed to help the
individual, irrespective of his age, make his way in
society. For the poor, these programs are designed
to develop a "sense of community" that does not presently exist in the ghetto. In essence, the community
action program is designed to enfranchise the poor
socially, politically, and educationally so that they
will later be able to become economically enfranchise
and thus be able to move into the mainstream of Amer-
can life. In other words, community action programs
are designed to provide them with the "sense of belonging" and the feeling of community cohesiveness
that is regarded as typifying the greater bulk of our
middle-class society. By providing them with this
sense of belonging, it is hoped that they will then
be motivated to avail themselves of existing social
services and manpower and skills training programs.
By developing their own internalized demand for socia
services and, hence, social progress, it is presumed
that they will be personally motivated to break out
of the culture of poverty in which they are now im-
mersed.

If this simplistic description of an anti-poverty
or Model Cities program is correct, it then follows
that there are two basic components of any complete
anti-poverty effort: (1) a set of production-oriente
skills and training programs designed to provide the
individual with those skills that will have a direct
bearing on his income producing ability, and (2) a
set of community-oriented or personal investment programs designed to develop an active demand within the
individual for these social welfare programs that
help motivate him to break out of the so-called culture of poverty. As experience has shown, manpower
and skill training programs by themselves are insufficient to the task. The individual participant suffers from too many other personal, social, and
environmental disabilities--poor health, an inadequat
basic education, poor family conditions, the efficier
cy or even the lack of a public transportation system
a sense of apathy--for the manpower and skills training program by itself to be optimally successful in
helping him to break out of the poverty cycle in whic

he finds himself. These other disabilities must be
cured or at least brought under control if the social
profit generated by a manpower and skills training
program is to be maximized.

From an administrative point of view then, continuing investments must be made in community organization and political action programs. Given our
present knowledge of human behavior and the present
state of the social sciences, these programs are the
only platform on which optimally successful manpower
and skills training programs can be mounted. Without a basic investment in the socialization and acculturation process--or the enfranchising as one of
us would have it--the foundations for long-term social
progress cannot be laid. Yet, these self-same basic
human resource programs do not have a readily observable output. Given the present state of our knowledge on the techniques for measuring the outputs of
these programs, one must accept a priori the notion
that these programs have an acceptable or measurable
output. At the present time a cost-benefit analysis
of their output would be discouraging unless we accept the hypothesis that these community organization
and social action programs are "overhead cost" that
must be tolerated because without them it is nigh
unto impossible to produce "profit-making" manpower
and skills training programs. Given this point of
view, a black workers program, for example, can be
viewed as an overhead cost, i.e., a marketing effort
that helps people to become aware of the social services that are available to them. This marketing
effort helps these people to develop their own internal demand for those types of social services that
will eventually motivate them to overcome their personal and communal disabilities. As they become accustomed to the process of buying these social
services and as they legitimate for themselves the
efficacy of these social services, it then becomes
possible to introduce into the community broader-based,
discipline-oriented manpower and skills training programs whose purpose it is to provide to the poor a
direct access to economic improvement. Because they
represent programs which produce direct and measurable
economic and financial benefits, the skills and

manpower training programs then become visible profit
makers for the total anti-poverty effort, i.e., they
are the hub of the variable cost of a system-wide
cost-effectiveness or cost-benefit analysis.

Thus, the 65:35 HRA funding split discussed
earlier in this section can be viewed as the outcome
of a series of decisions which states that $65 must
be invested in community overhead--black workers,
multi-service centers, health care, Head Start, remedial education, or similar programs--for every $35
invested in production-oriented variable-cost manpowe
and skills training programs. In the case of the
HRA, there is no guarantee that the 65:35 split was
or is rational. Indeed, the state of our knowledge
of the devices and programs capable of breaking the
cycle of poverty is such that no normative statement
can now be made on an optimal split between community
oriented and economically-oriented programs.

The point at issue is that there is a basic overhead cost implicit in every anti-poverty program, and
that an explicit sum of money must be devoted to thes
overhead costs before additional sums--the variable
costs--can be meaningfully invested in production-
oriented (output) programs. Also at issue is our
perception of the need for linking manpower and skill
training programs to basic human investment programs.
We believe that there may be an optimal balance between a basic human investment program and a
production-oriented program. Although we are not now
able to to hazard any guess on this balance, we would
maintain that the fixed cost-variable cost form of
analysis allows for a first approximation of this op-
timizing split. It does so because the total anti-
poverty program has a cost structure that can
meaningfully be subdivided into two parts:

(1) The overhead cost or fixed cost represented by the community organization, the political action program or any set of programs whose output is
concerned with the socialization, acculturation, or
enfranchising process.

(2) The variable cost represented by the manpower skills and training program--or any other program that is production- or output-oriented.

Similarly, this total package of programs has a total output. Some of these outputs or benefits can be stated in financial terms; some cannot. Those programs whose benefits can be monetized provide the initial basis for an analysis of the over-all monetary benefit provided by the aggregate portfolio of antipoverty programs. At the present time, we would maintain that this first approximation is the best that can be obtained in a cost-benefit analysis of an antipoverty program. However, even this first approximation of cost and benefits is a major step forward in the planning process if the decision-maker recognizes that the mathematics of this first approximation are based upon the presumed existence of a production function for the output of essential social services. This first approximation is made even more vital if an attempt is made to quantify the nonmonetized outputs of the funds devoted to overhead cost and, in doing so, determine the relative efficiency of this segment of the Model Cities program. This is the subject of the next section of this chapter.

NATURAL GROUPS

A recent study of Boston's West End by Herbert Gans entitled "The Urban Villagers" indicated that there are a number of smaller enclaves of social groups within our large metropolitan areas and that these groups exist out of the mainstream of the society that surrounds them. Although Gans thought of the urban villagers in terms of their ethnic origins, it is also possible to codify these groups according to those personal characteristics which create these natural groupings. Thus an area where beatniks, homosexuals or addicts live represents a natural community of people whose social behavior is regarded as deviant. At the same time, natural groupings may be

determined by age, i.e., "all males aged 20-25," or
by some disability, i.e., "all the unemployed." Or
a natural group may be defined by a reasonable combination of the above, i.e., "an unemployed Spanish-
speaking drug addict between the ages of 20-25."

Gans' discussion of the urban villagers or the
"natural community" as we preferred to call it, suggested a way out of some of the basic dilemma surrounding the planning process.

(1) By defining a natural group, it is possible
to close in on the characteristics of the target
group for whom a program is to be developed. To the
extent that these characteristics can be validly defined, it is possible to develop a differentiated
product suited to their specific needs.

(2) By defining a natural grouping, it is also
possible to subdivide program structures so that they
can deal with meaningfully sized segments of the community. This problem is particularly critical in New
York City because of the fact that more than 900,000
people live in the three designated Model Cities areas

(3) By defining a natural grouping, it is also
possible to deal individually with groups for whom
special attention is desired.

Conversely, the recognition of the existence of
natural groupings of people with peculiar or idiosyncratic characteristics and needs means that the master
plan for an area must also have a series of sub-plans.
These sub-plans must directly relate to the existence
of these natural communities of people and to their
extraordinary requirements. For example, an educational program in the Bedford-Stuyvesant area of New
York should recognize the different language requirements of the Spanish-speaking Puerto Rican population
and the English-speaking Negro population. For purposes of an educational program which has language
skills as its ultimate purpose, the natural grouping
would then be (1) the Spanish-speaking population
and (2) the English-speaking American Negro. Conversely, a day-care center to be developed in the area

would have as its natural community "mothers with
dependent children between the ages of 0 and 7 years
of age."

To some extent, the notion of a life cycle hypothesis, basic and support programs, and the natural
groupings of people allows for programs of greater
visibility to be developed if visibility is desired.
At the same time, by identifying clearly the recipients of certain programs, these planning constructs
will also allow the benefits of the Model Cities program either to be diffused over a large segment of
the population or to be concentrated in a few. The
notion of diffusion or concentration of programmatic
structures is, of course, the determination or expression of a political value. Although he is responsible
for responding to specific political requirements,
expressing these values is not the function of the
planner.

Thus, the life cycle hypothesis, the basic and
support program concept, and the notion of a natural
community are ways of making clear the value judgments and the senses of priorities that are an essential part of the planning process. In our opinion,
these tools allow value judgments and priorities to
be set out in an explicit manner so that the political planners who are ultimately responsible for a
social welfare program can fully understand the im-
plication of their action. In addition, these explicit statements of goals, functions, values and
priorities invite the active and cognitive participation of the target population.

Taken together, these three notions or planning
constructs also pinpoint one of the most critical de-
fects in our planning process to date: the vagaries
of federal funding, and the start-stop nature of so
many social welfare programs. Because of these two
factors, as a society we have not had sufficient time
to develop a truly rehabilitative social service
mechanism: one that will truly enable the culturally
and economically deprived to find their way into a
full partnership with the rest of our society. By
making evident the full range of the needs of an

individual over the total structure of his life, and
by looking for evidence of shortcomings in the social
service delivery system in the community, we hoped to
take a first valid step forward in overcoming these
shortcomings. Critical to the whole issue, of course
is the ability to use existing delegate agencies for
existing societal needs. This means that their program structures must be classified either according
to the taxonomy that we have suggested or a reasonabl
substitute for this taxonomy. However, it must be
recognized that any inventory of existing resources
will yield the same answer: There are insufficient
resources for the substantial unfilled needs in our
society. At the same time, however, it is reasonably
evident that many of the delegate agencies can be
made more efficient if their program structures are
linked together so that those agencies with basic
programs can be helped by those agencies that provide
support programs. It is of course assumed that the
Model Cities legislation is designed to create this
type of synergistic coordination once societal needs
and existing resources are properly identified.

FREEDOM OF CHOICE AND THE "TRANSMISSION BELT" CONCEPT

The two final statements of understanding that
we developed in our planning efforts were those of
the "freedom of choice" and the "transmission belt"
concept. In general, the people in a Model Cities
area can set for themselves one of two mutually exclusive goals:

(1) The goal of improving their personal capabilities and potential so that they can if desired
move out of the ghetto and into a more desirable part
of the city or the suburbs, or

(2) The goal of improving the environment in
which they now live, i.e., the ghetto, so that this
area becomes for them their first choice of an environment for themselves and for their children.

If the first goal is accepted, the Model Cities
program can then be regarded as a transmission belt

onto which a massive input of services, programs, and
technical skills is placed for the purpose of upgrading an individual's potentials in order to provide
him with the upward mobility that he needs to escape
the ghetto. As these rehabilitated residents move
out of the ghetto, others in their former condition
can be encouraged to move in, take part in the programmatic structure, and similarly escape their substandard environment.

At the other end of the spectrum of Model Cities
goals is that of the improvement and the stabiliza-
tion of the ghetto so that those who decide to remain
may enjoy the same quality of life as those who decide to leave. Clearly these two goals dictate a
different set of programs and a different set of priorities for those natural communities that now live
within the ghetto. The philosophy underlying these
two different approaches is significantly different.
Because of this philosophic difference, it was out
perception that the Model Cities resident should be
permitted to exercise his personal freedom of choice
as it affected his decision to either remain or not
remain in the ghetto. We assumed that a thousand individual choices would add up to an evident trend and
this trend would eventually be adopted by the community.

We also assumed that the programmatic structure
of the Model Cities program would be altered to fit
these different perceived needs although this might
create some fractionating inefficiencies within the
total program. Last, we assumed that the participation of the poor in the planning process would provide the platform around which the various natural
groupings in the community could coalesce and, in so
doing, assert their own preference on the nature of
the Model Cities process.

It is evident that if people in the target area
adopt the transmission belt concept, that the emphasis on planning must then be on task-type programs.
By task-type programs we mean those programs that
emphasize manpower, industrial development and other
supporting services primarily geared to producing a
higher income for the recipient. In this case, a
minimum of attention can be given to those programs

that emphasize community cohesiveness and community
organization programs since the individual intends
to leave that community.

Conversely, if the alternative of a stabilized
ghetto community is desired, this means that
maintenance-type programs must be given first priority. By maintenance programs, we mean those that
emphasize community organization factors; cultural,
religious, and recreational activities that tie a
community together are examples of this type of programmatic structure. Once these basic programs designed to develop a sense of community are underway,
support programs such as work skills programs can
then be introduced into the target area. Thus, the
dichotomy between the transmission belt concept and
the "separate but equal" society concept becomes
evident only in the redefinition of what constitutes
a basic or a support program. For the transmission
belt concept, manpower and skills training programs
are the basic programs. For the "separate but equal"
society, the community organization program is the
basic program. The changing of priorities provides
for the differing desires of different natural communities or target groups. Although the change in
emphasis may not be a pervasive change, the change
is nonetheless real.

In reality, the goals of a Model Cities program
cannot be this clear-cut. The goals and the programmatic structure that flow from these goals must represent a mixture of both types of program goals.
Over time, however, one type of goal will receive
more attention than another as the predominant desire
of the community becomes known. For example, if the
Model Cities legislation had been implemented in the
early 1960's, the odds are that the transmission belt
concept would have been its dominant theme. In the
early 60's the civil rights movement believed that
all minority groups should be encouraged to move out
of the ghetto and into other parts of the city and
suburban areas. Over the past few years, however,
the civil rights movement has moved away from the
notion of an equal and integrated society and towards
the notion of an equal but separate society. To the

extent that this represents the real desire of the
black community, the emphasis in community action
programs should shift toward programs designed to improve the ghetto and the quality of life that one ob-
tains in the ghetto. Based on a 65:35 split in its
appropriations, New York City can be regarded as
responding to this form of community pressure. At
the same time, the HRA because of its manpower component can be regarded as accommodating the desires
of those persons who want to escape the ghetto. However, one caveat should be observed: No real presumption can be made on the true rationality of the HRA
program because little is known of the decision-
making process that created the 65:35 split. Pre-
sumptively, it was a decision made after a thorough
analysis of the trade-offs involved between community
maintenance and community development programs. At
the same time, it must be recognized that the decision may have been a reactive one in response to a
set of political, social, and organizational realities that bear no cogent relevance to the needs of
the population that is to be served by the Model
Cities program. There are many economic, social,
and political barriers to the development of comprehensive social welfare programs. Although these can
be dismissed as irrelevant to an academic discussion
of the planning process, they are critically relevant
to the real existence of Model Cities programs. Unless the community at large understands and supports
these socially oriented programs, they will not receive the public support that is essential to their
success. The planner must be able to show the public
at large what is being done, and the overall benefit
to society of these programs. Not until this is done
will he have completed the planning process as we
view it. Legitimation is essential.

In order to accomplish all of this, however, the
planner needs a kit of tools that allows him to explicate the planning process. Our work in New York
City led us to the belief that the life cycle hypothesis provides a way for explaining and interpreting
to the public the planning efforts underlying a Model
Cities program. By refining the administrative process to include the notions of the natural community,

the basic and support program, and the fixed and
variable cost factors underlying the rationalization
of a program structure, we believe that we developed
a technique for making explicit the actions that we
proposed to take, and the basic reasons for these
actions. If, indeed, this is true, an anti-poverty
program can then be explained to the population it
is supposed to serve and they can then actively participate in the planning process by altering its
goals, emphasis, and priorities to fit their own perception of their own needs. A basis for informed
action will have been provided to them and the planning process will then have become a valid exercise
in participatory democracy because the desires of
those affected by legislation will affect the interpretation of this legislation.

CRITERIA FOR SELECTION OF PROGRAM GOALS

Within each of the two goals orientations that
we have suggested as appropriate for the Model Cities
program, a vast variety of programs and programmatic
structures are possible. Because of this, we recognized that criteria must be developed for ranking
individual programs. The Model Cities legislation
itself provides some principles from which criteria
may be developed. The criteria that we developed for
the New York Model Cities program are presented below. The definition of the key terms used in these
criteria will be found in Appendix A. Appendix B
shows the ranking process as it applied to a number
of ongoing HRA programs.

(1) Model Cities funds should be used only in
the Model Cities area if at all possible.

(2) Model Cities programs should be related
directly to ongoing urban renewal or vest-pocket
housing projects.

(3) Priority should be given to programs that
can be quickly mounted if new, or quickly expanded
if already in existence.

(4) A program should be capable of gathering additional resources (capital, buildings, technical personnel) from the private sector.

(5) A program should be highly desired by the people of the natural community that it is designed to serve.

(6) Programs that contain both rehabilitative (task oriented) and preventative (community maintenance) components should be emphasized, particularly in the first years of the Model Cities program.

(7) Programs that directly utilize the services of the poor in either policy-making or staff positions should be emphasized.

(8) Programs that reinforce each other as opposed to those that exist in isolation should be emphasized.

As shown in Appendix B, these criteria were used to rank a number of existing and projected HRA and Model Cities programs. One point was given for a program that appeared to meet a criterion fully, one half point for a program that met a criterion partially, and zero score for a program that did not meet the criterion at all. The total points earned by each of the programs are shown below. The individual rating given a program for each of the eight criteria are presented in Appendix B. Some of the programs for which the criteria were tested fell into a functional classification that could be the responsibility of the HRA, the HDA, or some other city agency. Only those programs which came to the attention of the Model Cities Coordinator were ranked. The ranking process itself is not precise nor can it ever be because a certain amount of judgment must be used during the scoring process. In the scoring model that we elected to use, eight points represented the highest rank possible, and zero points the lowest.

Eight Points

(1) Neighborhood manpower centers
(2) Mini-bussing (to places of work and business)
(3) Housing office with rental information

Seven and One-Half Points

(4) Community corporations
(5) Cooperative housing for low-income families

Seven Points

(6) Multi-service centers
(7) Mobile medical-dental units for the home-bound

Six and One-Half Points

(8) Vocational education in schools after hours
(9) Residential youth center
(10) Housing office to assist newcomers in their adjustment to the community
(11) Housing workshop clinic (improve tenant-owner relationships and maintenance of property)
(12) Industry's use of special schools or classrooms to test out their developing teaching devices
(13) Two-year community colleges

Six Points

(14) Scheuer program (manpower training for public sector jobs)
(15) Career ladder concepts
(16) Use of older adults to supervise youths in recreational activities
(17) Early childhood programs
(18) Development of health centers
(19) Creation of a center of innovation (children, pre-kindergarten to second grade)
(20) Street workers program
(21) Street academies

Five and One-Half Points

(22) Concentrated employment programs
(23) Encouragement of business and industry to develop training programs for low-income persons

Five Points

(24) Youth employment service
(25) Legal services for the poor

Four to Four and One-Half Points

(26) Family planning clinics
(27) Welfare center
(28) Emergency temporary housing pool
(29) Small business assistance office

Two and One-Half to Three and One-Half Points

(30) Job counseling
(31) No-bail projects
(32) Twenty-four-hour court sessions
(33) A central data bank

If the criteria listed above were indeed the only basis for ranking Model Cities programs, it would then follow that those programs with the highest point total should be implemented. However, other considerations may determine whether or not a program with a lower score should be given precedence over one with a higher score. Feasibility, the projected effectiveness of the program, and the political acceptability of the program itself are examples of other such factors that must be evaluated before a final decision is made on which programs will be funded and which will not.

GUIDELINES FOR PACKAGING PROGRAMS

Once the priority given to achieve a series of goals has been determined, the next step in the process is to bring together into a program a whole series

of basic and support projects. Some of these programs will be expensive, others less so. For example,
it may cost $1 million to establish a counseling ser-
vice or an Opportunity Service Unit and less than
$25,000 to establish and maintain a data bank for
tracking job openings and trainees capable of filling
those openings. The various packages to be presented
to the target area population should, of course, be
consistent with the total sum that can be generated
by the Model Cities program. HUD officials expect
$9 to be generated for every $1 of Model Cities supplemental funds granted to a city.

The following guidelines are suggested as a means
for accomplishing the packaging process.

(1) The package should be directly related to
those categories in the life cycle in which the main
programmatic emphasis is to be placed. This emphasis
should be the results of a series of decisions made
by the appropriate political groups; i.e., the city
administration, the representatives of the poor, delegate agency representatives, etc.

(2) The component parts of each package should
be flexible enough to be interchanged with parts of
other packages.

(3) Many alternative packages of programs
should be developed so that the decision-making group
will be accorded the maximum amount of freedom in the
selection of programs and packages of programs.

(4) The component parts of the package should
be relevant to two or more of the specified objectives
of the Model Cities program.

(5) A description of the component parts of
each program or package should contain, at minimum,
the following information:

(a) The approximate cost to serve 1,000
persons, e.g.: (1) A manpower program
may require $400,000 to serve 1,000
persons at $400 per trainee; (2) An

out-reach program requires $50,000 to
serve 1,000 persons.

(b) The type of staffing pattern required
even if the exact number is not available, e.g.: Two Opportunity Service
Units to serve 1,000 families requires
social workers, trained indigenous
staff and clerical staff. If exact
numbers were available, this would show
two social work supervisors, ten Opportunity Service Unit workers and four
clerks.

(c) The relationship with other programs
and/or agencies which are required to
make the program work, e.g.: Training
welfare mothers depends on a cooperative
relationship with MCDA, CDA, unions,
and hospitals.

(d) The approximate amount of resources
(facilities, staff and financing) now
available from current allocations, and
the new resources needed from Model
Cities funds or elsewhere to put the
programs into operation.

(e) The changes in laws, regulations, practices, administrative operations or the
structural set-up of the programs need
to permit them to become operational.

(f) The target population for the program,
and the rationale for choosing this
target population.

(g) Any anticipated negative effect that
the programs may have on existing activities and a statement indicating how
the expected positive gains will out-
weigh these effects.

A sample package might include the following components. The target population for this package is

1,000 welfare mothers, aged 18-26, for whom a skills training program is to be developed.

SAMPLE PACKAGE

	Cost per 1,000
Basic Programs	
Manpower service center	$ 50,000
Skill center	1,500,000
Support Programs	
Mini-bussing	300,000
Special services (multi-service center) average $200/case	200,000
ADC child care (living room)	1,200,000
Head Start	1,200,000
Recreation center	250,000
Health services ($50/case)	50,000
Housing clinic	50,000
Legal services	200,000
	$5,000,000

It is obvious that both of these techniques--that for ranking individual programs and the technique for packaging a set of programs--needs much refinement. However, the methods that we have suggested once agai point to a way for delving meaningfully into the plan ning process. Clearly, a cost-benefit or a cost-effectiveness analysis of an individual program or package of programs will help to make the decision-making process, and the rationale for this process, more explicit. However, after all is said and done, political and social realities must also be accounted for in the Model Cities process. By altering the rank ing process to suit these realities, program ranking procedures can be changed to suit the expressed needs of the target population and all others involved in the Model Cities process. Once again, the key ration ale for the techniques that we have suggested is the need for making explicit the planning process and the

system of societal values that underlie this process.
We have not presumed to determine these values although the examples we used did, of necessity, encom-
pass certain value judgments.

CHAPTER **4** CITIZEN PARTICIPATION

Chapter 1 presented the background history that has led to the present emphasis in federal legislation for increasing participation of the poor in those programs that directly affect them. Chapters 2 and 3 described reality factors in planning Model Cities and a planning concept that was proposed for New York City. In that concept, the role of the citizen was alluded to. The next two chapters will analyze in some detail the complexities and implications of citizen participation.

This chapter will be divided into the following sections:

(1) The definition, role, and implications of citizen participation;
(2) Models for citizens' organization structures;
(3) Relationship of citizen bodies to public and private sectors;
(4) Inter- and intra-organizational conflicts that affect the citizen's role; and
(5) Other factors that affect citizen activity.

The major hypothesis that governs the discussion in this chapter is that it is not possible to pre-scribe in advance how citizens in any one community should be organized and involved in the planning of Model Cities. On the other hand, it does accept the notion that the poor have not been influential in the passage or interpretation of laws that have primarily affected them. Since a law and its manner of imple-mentation are largely the product of political lever-age, the poor with their minimal influence have been

excluded from this process until very recently, and
then included only in a token way. One of the objectives of both the anti-poverty and Model Cities
programs has been to strengthen this representation.
The main aim of this chapter is to identify the complex nature of citizen participation and some of the
factors and implications of this involvement.

DEFINITION, ROLE, AND IMPLICATIONS OF
CITIZEN PARTICIPATION

In recent years, there has been a growing insis-
tence on the part of the residents of the poverty
areas that they be involved in the planning and implementation of programs that affect them. At the
same time, the response on the part of the federal
government has been to support this demand by the
passage of two legislative acts, the Economic Opportunity Act of 1964 and the Demonstration Cities Act
of 1966. The precedent for this trend of increasing
citizen involvement is found in the administration
of the Federal Housing Act of 1949, as amended in
1954, and the historic Supreme Court decisions of
1954, and the civil rights actions which were attempts to enforce it. These events have set in mo-
tion a drive by the poor for their demanding a voice
in determining the nature of programs that directly
affect them. They have increasingly charged local
municipal officials with denying them a role in the
decision-making process as mandated by the federal
acts. Yet, when one refers to these acts, none of
them precisely spells out what that role should be.
Nor is this possible because the very nature of citizen involvement is quite complex and therefore open
to many interpretations depending on the perspective
from which one views this.

The basic discussion in this section will focus
on two key elements inherent in the nature of citizen
participation. The first section will be devoted to
identifying "who" has been involved in the past. The
second will discuss some of the basic functions citizens can and have taken on in programs stressing
citizen participation. This analysis will then

consider the implications of the demand for greater
involvement by low-income residents.

The Class of Citizens

"Who" is involved in citizen activity is often
a function of whose interest is at stake. In early
urban renewal projects, only the citizen elite were
involved. These early renewal projects concentrated
on revitalizing central business districts, and saw
only the need for involving those whose resources
were needed to redevelop the area. This generally
included business, newspaper, church, and university
interests. Those who were adversely affected by the
project, usually by being displaced, had no voice and
were not even given the courtesy of an advisory role
in decision making. However, when in the 1960's urban renewal began its shift to residential rehabilitation, the neighborhood leaders (settlement house
directors, church leaders, local store owners, and
leaders of neighborhood associations), previously
ignored in prior planning efforts, became the main
citizen participants. And many of these neighborhood
leaders were also invited to serve on the city-wide
boards.

In the anti-poverty program, a similar pattern
developed in many of the community action agencies
(CAA). Whether in large cities where both city-wide
and neighborhood CAA boards were formed (as in Boston
Philadelphia, and New York), or in smaller cities
with one CAA board, city-wide leaders found their way
onto the larger boards; neighborhood elite, onto the
smaller ones. The neighborhood boards tended to reflect the substantive concerns of their constituency
(better housing, job training, and so forth) whereas
city-wide boards tended to reflect procedural concerns (procuring and allocating funds, board make-up,
and balancing demands made on it). Whether the board
members were elected or appointed, neighborhood leaders, who were not usually classified economically as
being members of the "poverty class," were usually
the representatives of the poor on these boards.

The federal guidelines for the Model Cities program have also emphasized the role of the local citiz

in the planning process. A survey of some of the
first municipal applications to obtain a planning
grant showed that the class of persons involved on
such planning councils will differ little from the
CAA boards, with the major exception that the city's
chief elected and appointed officials will probably
have the major decision-making voice. Like the recent changes in the OEO Act, Model Cities guidelines
call for a partnership among the city's political
leaders, its institutional leaders, and Model Cities
neighborhood leaders.

The Model Cities program is the most comprehensive governmental thrust yet devised to revitalize
the poverty areas. As such, it must necessarily
touch the widest spectrum of different interest groups
whose interests will be affected by it. In addition
to the leadership of the anti-poverty agencies in the
areas, a number of other groups have demanded some
voice in the planning. Among these are city-wide
public and private groups such as health and welfare
councils, chambers of commerce, boards of education,
mental health bodies and the newly created urban co-
alitions. Many of these city-wide bodies have local
counterparts operating in Model Cities areas. They
too want to be represented. Among these are the local family agencies, YMCAs, real estate boards, businessmen's associations, and local planning boards.
Other important bodies with a stake in Model Cities
planning are the local store front and established
churches and the local political bodies. Finally,
there are classes of people who are either poorly
represented by organized groups or have no spokesmen
at all. Among these are the small homeowners, numerous small local businessmen, the elderly, welfare
recipients, neighborhood tenant associations, and
many of those who lost out in the anti-poverty elec-
tions.

A number of issues arise with respect to how these
diverse groups will participate in the planning process. How will the Model Cities planning body be
structured in the community? How much power will be
delegated to the different interest groups? How will
they be selected? Who decides who will be selected?
It is around attempts to answer questions such as

these that a number of conflicts have developed within the Model Cities areas. These questions will be taken up in a later section of this chapter.

In the past fifteen years, basic federal laws and their amendments have been increasingly specific in determining "who" should be involved in planning and implementing those programs on the local scene. As the poor have become more aware of the stakes involved and sophisticated in the art and use of power, their participation has become more widespread. This has been especially true in the Model Cities program.

As the federal government has balanced its concern for physical and economic rehabilitation of the cities with growing emphasis on the revitalization and enhancement of the social fabric of the poor, two trends come to light. First, the programs designed to assist the residents of these areas have become more geographically concentrated and programmatically comprehensive. The Model Cities program is by far more comprehensive and concentrated in its intent than either the urban renewal or anti-poverty programs that preceded it.

Second, the federal regulations of these three programs have been more explicit in defining a planning policy and implementing role for the poor. However, they have balanced this by insisting that city officials and local civic institutions with a stake in the poverty areas also be included. Thus, the current emphasis in the Model Cities program is on a balanced partnership of all classes of local leadership in sharp contrast to the unbalanced citizen bodies that constituted previous local boards that guided federal programs in the poverty areas. The shift toward balanced participation has come about out of a recognition that the poverty neighborhood and the city as a whole are intimately dependent on each other. Local and city-wide leadership are both needed to bring about rebuilding and integration of slum areas with the rest of the city.

Functions of Citizen Participants

A study of the federal acts and a review of pertinent literature reveals that there are five basic functions which citizens can potentially perform. These are:

(a) Planning the program
(b) Setting policy with decision-making power
(c) Sanctioning programs or policies
(d) Helping in the initial implementation of the program
(e) Staffing and operating the program

Planning as a Citizen Function

There are many ways in which the citizen can be involved in the planning function. At one extreme, he can actually plan his own programs as the community action programs have demonstrated. In Boston's South End Urban Renewal Projects, residents in the sixteen sub-areas that made up the project were heavily involved in the actual planning of their neighborhoods with the technical assistance of professional planning staff. As the other extreme, the citizen can act as a sounding or advisory board to a planning agency which has created its own plan. In this capacity, the citizen body offers recommendations for improvements in the plan which the planning agency is free to accept or reject. Urban renewal planning in Newark was largely on this order. The citizen's planning function was held to a minimum.

A mid-ground position calls for the citizen body to choose from among a series of alternative options designed to meet his needs as perceived by the planner. Then, in negotiations with city officials and other interested parties, one of these options is jointly agreed upon. This type of citizen planning took place in Boston's Washington Park Urban Renewal Project in the early 1960's and most recently in New York City's Vest Pocket Housing Program in 1967.

For citizens to plan themselves, they need to have access to technical expertise which is sympathetic to their way of viewing things, or the funds to hire their own planners. Model Cities planning grants make this latter option a real possibility. A number of cities have used the planning grant in this way. The current trend toward more community control implies a greater movement in citizen-initiated planning. Without the citizens having access to their own planners, they must rely on the compromise option of reacting to a series of alternative options offered to them by the administering agency. This is the dominant method of citizen involvement today and implies a partnership of trust and confidence of the citizen in the sincerity of city agencies and their planners. In too many instances, this mutual trust is lacking, which is a partial reason why citizens are insisting on hiring their own planners.

There are many variations on these three methods for citizen planning. Political power and the community's traditional way of organizing itself and doing business with city officials are often the compelling factors in determining the degree of citizen involvement in planning.

Decision-making as a Citizen Function

The decision-making function refers to the degree of authority given to a citizen body to render final decisions over programs and policies in which it has a vital stake. At one end of the continuum, citizen bodies can be given advisory responsibilities only. The city-wide urban renewal boards in Boston and New Haven held this type of limited authority. Their powers came from their capacity to influence the real decision-makers (the city council and the urban renewal agency) through informal means. This is the most limited type of decision-making function. And it is the kind that the leaders of poverty communities have come to reject as being ritualistic rather than real.

On the other hand, the citizen body can be given formal authority to make binding policy and program decisions. This is most true of the current community action agencies where the citizen boards have the power and authority to allocate funds, decide on priorities and set general policy.

A mid-ground between these extremes is represented by a citizen body that has its authority in decision-making prescribed by a higher policy body. Within the policy limits set by this higher body, it has the authority to act autonomously. For example, in New York City's Council Against Poverty, the city-wide CAP council is the body that sets general policy and allocates OEO funds for New York City's 26 designated poverty areas. Within the CAP policy and its financial limits, the neighborhood CAAs have many options to execute programs desired by the residents. This mid-ground implies that all authority is in essence relative to some higher governing body. Thus, even where a citizen body has authority to make certain decisions at the neighborhood level, it may discover that the programs it has planned may bear little resemblance to those finally approved at higher governmental levels. Or it may find those programs rejected altogether. In early 1968, President Johnson's shifting of OEO funds to adult training programs resulted in many programs already approved by neighborhood and municipal CAAs being cut back or abandoned. The decision-making role of the citizen in Model Cities planning must of necessity be of this type because it is not possible for a city administration to delegate all of its authority to a local citizen body. The numerous issues resulting from such a decision-making role are discussed in a later section of this chapter.

Sanctioning as a Citizen Function

Sanctioning refers to the approval that is given or withheld by one individual or group to the formal acts desired or performed by another individual or group. It represents a form of informal citizen power, but carries no official authority behind the act of endorsement or rejection. Sanctioning is the step that usually occurs prior to the official enactment of a public program. It takes many forms. Anonymous letters to newspapers and participating in polls

or surveys represent two of the least personal forms
of sanctioning a program. On the other hand, lobby-
ing and making speeches before public bodies are two
of the most active and personal ways of an individual
or group expressing its opinions about a program.
When 90 per cent of the citizen organizations and
leaders of Boston's South End expressed support for
an urban renewal program proposed for their area, the
official decision-making bodies (the Boston Redevelopment Authority and the Boston City Council) received
the message that they should approve this program in
spite of the ambivalence expressed by some of their
members toward the project. Both bodies eventually
supported the project by comfortable voting margins.
In contrast, 90 per cent of the residents in Boston's
Charlestown section expressed strong disapproval of
a similar program in a public hearing. It subsquent-
ly took the renewal agency another two years of intensive effort to correct the criticisms directed at
its plan in order to gain the community's sanction
and eventual Council endorsement.

Sanctioning of a public program is much more
difficult to achieve among aroused than apathetic
citizens. Public disapproval by the potential bene-
ficiaries of a program such as urban renewal or Model
Cities is a powerful weapon citizen bodies have at
their disposal to influence the official decision-
makers. It may, in fact, represent a more important
citizen function than that of actual decision making.
However, sanctioning represents a reaction to decisions someone else has already made or is about to
make. It implies a citizen participation after the
fact which is in fact only the power of rubber-
stamping a plan. In today's atmosphere, Model Cities
residents will most likely look unfavorably upon programs which they have had no part in developing.
Sanctioning will not be seen by them as a separate
or valuable function, but as a function to be carried
out through their own planning and decision-making.

Initial Implementation as a Citizen Function

Once a program has been endorsed and officially
enacted, it must be implemented to serve the people

for whom it is designed. Implementation as used in
this context is the process of converting a plan into a working program with the necessary physical
facilities and personnel to run it. It does not refer to the everyday administration of a program. An
example of this function is a community action program that is initiated in a neighborhood. Usually
a citizen committee will assume the initial responsibility for finding a store front, recruiting and ap-
pointing a director, and publicizing the program.
In this way, a citizen body performs an initial implementing function by getting a program started.
The citizen body can either carry out this initial
function itself or delegate it to hired staff which
executes it under the citizens' supervision. In today's atmosphere of suspicion, programs perceived as
being "imposed" on the poverty area residents from
the outside are often rejected or underutilized. But
the involvement of citizen leaders in the initiation
of new programs serves the crucial purpose of insuring their better acceptance by the community because
they are viewed as their own.

Furthermore, local citizens, when permitted to
collaborate with city officials in the initial implementation of governmental programs, can offer valuable
guidance to city officials on site selection of facilities, recruitment of indigenous staff, and more
acceptable procedures for rendering service. Local
citizens are particularly equipped for this through
their awareness of the unique cultural and environmental factors that must be taken into account. Finally, their involvement in initiating such programs
as half-way houses for addicts or alcoholics, or community mental health facilities is especially important because of the ambivalent attitudes local
residents have toward persons needing such services.
Though many residents would prefer not having such
facilities in their community, they are more accepting of these when they are planned and run by local
residents whom they know and trust. Thus, how a
program created to assist low-income residents is
initiated becomes important. And it therefore becomes important to have some citizen involvement in
the beginning phases of these programs to insure their

getting off to a successful start in order to better
meet the real needs of people.

Administration as a Citizen Function

Administration refers to those procedures and
policies required to carry out a program on a day-
to-day basis once it has been launched. One does not
ordinarily think of citizens being involved in this
type of function but in the poverty areas this has
become an increasingly important citizen function for
several reasons. First, the users of current health,
welfare, and educational services are vehemently critical of how they are administered. Too often the
poor suffer from the way these programs are administered on a day-to-day basis. For this reason, they
are demanding a role in the operation and restructuring of these programs. The organized efforts of welfare mothers and the struggle of local citizen groups
with New York City's Board of Education are two such
endeavors to gain some control over these programs.
And one of the demands they are making is to gain the
power to appoint principals and other administrative
officials.

Second, the leaders among the citizen groups in
the low-income areas have been projected into senior
administrative positions in many of the community action and manpower training programs. Through their
position on the policy-making boards or as "behind
the scenes" power brokers, they have influence over
such administrative decisions as staffing and hiring
patterns, promotions, salary increases, strategy for
obtaining increased funds from governmental and private sources, and determining whom the program will
serve. In these ways, the citizens who placed these
leaders in their positions continue to exert a direct
influence in determining how these programs are administered.

Third, both new and existing programs are increasingly becoming training grounds for starting the
under-educated, under-trained poor on "career ladders
that lead to increasingly responsible positions com-
mensurate with their on-the-job training, formal

education, and innate capacities. Citizen groups
are often active in both demanding such training programs and recruiting local residents to fill the
training vacancies. Once they have become involved
in these activities, they also try to influence their
daily operations. Citizen bodies have therefore become more insistent in playing a role in every facet
of new programs started in their behalf. As a result
of these community pressures, new opportunities are
also opening up in the more established municipal
programs such as health, welfare, police, and sanitation departments. It is expected that the advent
of the Model Cities program will tend to accelerate
the influence citizen bodies will demand in the administration of such basic programs.

This brief discussion identifies some of the possible functions which citizen have played and will
continue to play in programs affecting them. Short
of the Model Cities areas becoming autonomous municipalities within the larger cities, there is no way
to know in advance which of these functions and the
variety of roles within them will be played by the
citizens, and which ones by the public and private
agencies. Regardless of how citizen participation
evolves in each community, the analysis of just these
five functions reveal how many-faceted the role of
citizen activity can be. Past experiences have revealed a number of implications that flow from citizen involvement. The next section will focus on some
of them.

Implications

CDA Letter No. 3 identified a number of general
functions requiring some degree of citizen involvement, but these were stated so generally as to permit
a wide range of interpretations on the part of the
CDA of the degree to which the citizen would be involved. In the past, city agencies have generally
given as little decision-making power to citizens as
they could get away with giving. Until the enactment of the Economic Opportunity Act, the poor were
seldom involved. Since then, their demands for gen-
uine citizen involvement have increased and been

rewarded with greater control over new programs that
affect them. The leaders of the poor in the Model
Cities areas have been maneuvering to control and/or
influence this program. At the same time, city officials are also aware of the potential influence such
a program can have on their numerous programs already
operating in these areas. As both parties act to
maximize control over the Model Cities program, it
can be anticipated that conflicts will take place.
Neighborhood leaders will attempt to increase their
power and control of the Model Cities program while
city officials will strive to maintain as much control as possible.

Thus, the complex nature of citizen involvement
does not allow even the explicit federal guidelines
of CDA Letter No. 3 to forestall the inevitable confrontations that are and will continue to take place
in the planning and implementation of the Model Cities
program.

Furthermore, the very nature of the decision-
making process in Model Cities is such that complete
influence over the direction of a Model Cities program
can only come about if the citizens control all of
the five basic functions discussed above. This means
that bodies in the Model Cities areas must be in a
position to control the whole process of involvement
or risk the programs being deflected in a direction
contrary to its best interests. However, it is obviously politically, economically, and administrative
ly impossible for this to happen in comprehensive
programs like the Model Cities program. City agencies
civic and voluntary agencies, and profit-making inter
ests have too much at stake to give up their interest
to citizen groups, whether city-wide or neighborhood
based.

Consequently, the many forces at work in the community arena make it impossible to structure in advance the nature of citizen activity. In the course
of negotiations, each city will arrive at its own
unique combination in determining who will participat
and how. No formula can govern the final outcome nor
will two municipalities end up with the same citizen

structure. This fact of life also means that no one can safely predict what the final outcome of any federal program will be once its planning is initiated at the local level.

Federal programs like the anti-poverty and Model Cities act represent vast new sources of power for the poor that are being injected into the poverty neighborhoods. It is only natural that, within these neighborhoods, conflicts will take place over the control of these new resources. In time, a few leaders will emerge victorious. Either they or their hand-picked representatives will serve on most of the executive boards and community committees to protect their new hard won interests. These same few leaders will be asked again and again to serve on more and more committees. As a result of this accretion of civic responsibilities, these leaders will become too overburdened to devote an adequate amount of time to each of their citizen commitments.

They furthermore will in time pay the prices of having too little time left to maintain the initial source of their power, the group(s) they once represented. What are the consequences that derive from this accretion of power?

First, it is common for city officials to question whom these leaders represent when they take positions on questions of importance. All too often they have no answer because they come to represent themselves. They become in fact leaders-at-large without a constituency to which they can refer for guidance and support.

Second, these community leaders lose their identity with the "poor" as they, by virtue of their leadership capacity, are propelled out of the role of the poor into that of the middle-income class with executive salaries derived from managing programs related to the poor. Yet, these are the leaders who continue to "represent the poor" although they no longer are poor and may no longer be emotionally identified with them or their problems. Although these leaders may technically meet the federal requirements as representatives of the poor, do they in fact really best represent them? If not, it seems essential that a mechanism be built into the citizen participation process to insure that these no longer representative leaders can be replaced in an orderly manner by bona fide leaders of the poor.

Third, this concentration of power often does not guarantee representation of all parties whose interests have been or will be severely affected by federal programs. The Model Cities program will have the most widespread impact on those who live in, serve, or profit from the Model Cities areas. In these areas, there can usually be found enclaves of home-owning, struggling lower-middle-class families. There are also to be found private social agencies, churches, and numerous small businesses owned in many instances by local families. All of these elements have a stake in what happens to the Model Cities areas. Yet, while the federal regulations tend to have a bias in favor of their involvement in the Model Cities program, in practice citizen leaders of the organized poor tend to determine who get involved.

Because the Model Cities program is potentially so far-reaching in its affect on people and facilities, it becomes essential for federal regulations to require each city to spell out formal grievance procedures. Such procedures do not formally exist now, although informally individuals and groups with enough influence have usually had avenues opened for them to be heard. Because so many of the poor are not sophisticated in the use of informal procedures, these should be formalized and well-publicized in the Model Cities areas.

Because such formal mechanisms do not generally exist, it is far more common for these aggrieved neighborhood forces to fight against programs that adversely affect them even though they may be beneficial to their neighbors. Too seldom are compromise worked out in the spirit of cooperation under circumstances where force and power are the only means available to redress a grievance.

In the final analysis, regardless of how each municipality defines for itself the nature of citizen participation, the basic question still must be answered. Will the programs planned and implemented by the resident citizens be any more effective and responsive to the needs of their fellow citizens than those created by federal and municipal agencies? There is little evidence at this time to bear out the contention that the poor really produce superior and more effective programs than the city agencies charged with this responsibility. A recent New York Times news item stated that one of the original planners of HARYOU, the heavily financed Harlem anti-poverty program, called that program a failure. On the other hand, there is ample evidence to show that the involvement of the poor does change the balance of power in their neighborhoods and results in their most adequate representation in programs that directly affect them.

While the above discussion shows that the poor cannot be expected to control all the programs that affect them, it can also be shown that in our pluralistic society no group has the power to control completely the destiny of its own affairs. The important point is that the poor are increasing their power so that they can negotiate with city-wide leaders on a much stronger and politically powerful basis than was the case prior to the anti-poverty program. And the federal mandate for neighborhood involvement can be expected to become stronger with the planning of the Model Cities program.

THE ORGANIZATION OF CITIZENS

The previous section centered on the questions of "who was involved" and "what tasks such involved citizens performed." This section turns to the question of how citizens can organize themselves to perform these tasks. Three basic structures will be discussed: the unitary, the federation, and the coalition. Some of the strengths and weaknesses of each will be discussed, in addition to a few interesting variations of these structures. Finally, judgments will be offered, where possible, of the circumstances in which each of these types of organization has the best chance for success.

Unitary Structure

In a unitary structure organization, authority resides at the top, either in the hands of one person or in an executive body. Policy decisions are binding on those in subordinate positions in the hierarchy. Control is centralized, as in our great corporations. However, studies in formal organization have pointed out that authority is not automatically accepted by subordinates, who have many informal mechanisms for subverting the intent of decisions with which they are in disagreement. The point at which the persons in authority must consciously exercise it through the use of sanctions is already an indication of some loss of control over their subordinates. Thus, while there is a chain of command one can point to in a unitary structure, ther is still no guarantee that decisions made at the top will be carried out by those lower in the hierarchy.

In a Model Cities program, where many different autonomous self-interest groups must come together to plan, it is unlikely that a unitary structure has much hope of developing except under the unusual circumstance where the groups are few in number and have common interests and values that permit the different groups to agree on common goals. There should be enough of a cooperative and trusting relationship among the independent organizations to enable their agreeing to priorities and the allocation of limited resources. These characteristics are normally found in such organizations as the League of Women Voters, local neighborhood organizations, or special-interest groups. Such a unitary structure was formed from autonomous groups in Boston's South End to plan an urban renewal project. There, a central organization was created to serve as the decision-making body for the 16 neighborhood organizations and numerous commercial, welfare and institutional bodies that were located within its boundaries. This was made possibl

because the leadership of the central body and that
of the constituent groups did have common values and
interests. As a result they were able to agree on
priorities and compromised differences.

However, the Model Cities program comprises many
more groups, has larger population areas, and must
take into account many more services than an urban
renewal project. Welfare, police, sanitation, fire,
health, education and religious services must be made
available to the residents. Social and athletic
groups, civic associations, local stores and shopping
areas are other services people require. Whereas
urban renewal projects touched upon some of these
services, Model Cities planning must, according to
law, involve all of these services if it is to create
a comprehensive plan to revitalize the area. The
broad range of services needed requires the involvement of a wide variety of private and public organizations and agencies which have traditionally rendered
such services. Their goals, priorities, constituencies, resources, and values must necessarily cover a
wide spectrum of interests. To form a unitary structure that places power in the hands of a few leaders
at the top is an inconceivable notion because the
priorities of one group of needed services will undoubtedly get greater emphasis than another. For example, housing, jobs, and education are receiving
greater attention in New York City than recreation,
health, and social welfare services. The public sector has greater power in planning Model Cities in
New York City than the private sector. Community
leaders connected with anti-poverty programs have
greater local power than do the more established public or private leaders of neighborhood services. The
interests of the blacks and Puerto Ricans receive more
attention than do those of the whites living in the
same area. To what extent can one anticipate that
those whose interests receive less attention will cooperate with those favored? Yet, the very nature of
a Model Cities program requires that such priorities
be set. The leadership of a unitary structure is
unable to make sufficient allowances for such differences, or to dampen the conflicting interests involved.

Even if a unitary structure is formed, its effectiveness in implementing its plan will be severely limited unless it finds special means to involve those interests which have been given lower priority or excluded by the leaders of that structure. This is difficult to accomplish where there are insufficient resources to meet both high and low priority objectives. Even if adequate resources were available, the varying approaches of organizations are often incompatible or even in conflict with each other. For example, one group emphasizes stricter discipline in the schools while another encourages fuller expression of feelings and ideas. A religious group wants to attack juvenile delinquency by emphasizing moral and religious teaching; a family agency stresses a non-directive, family therapy approach; a third approach emphasizes job training and improved education. Just such confrontations over different ways to solve the problem will be encountered in Model Cities planning.

The very nature of the interests that must be involved in such planning are too widely divergent to enable one group to give up a part of its authority to a central decision-making body as required in a unitary structure. The best compromise that groups with their own integrity and self-interest to maintain can hope for is to find areas of agreement within functional committees such as housing, education, or transportation. Finding agreement on the committee level, however, in no way resolves the problem of how one allocates scarce resources among the various functional goals, how the priorities are arrived at, or how one resolves goal conflicts. There are too many dangers involved for autonomous groups to subordinate their authority to a unitary decision-making structure.

Numerous studies have pointed to the fact that there are many power centers in our cities and that no one group is so powerful that it can control what decisions will be made. The very essence of Model Cities planning calls for a coming together of these many power blocks. Therefore, given the nature of our pluralistic power centers and the need of Model Cities planning to coordinate these power blocks, it can almost be stated as a basic principle that an effective unitary structure will not be a feasible vehicle for planning

Federation

A federation is an organization in which authority is lodged in the constituent bodies that compose
it. Within broad guidelines previously agreed upon,
limited authority is delegated through representatives
to an executive committee and director to represent
the general interests of all the constituent members
in matters of common concern. Many city-wide organizations have formed variations of the federation
structure. Community councils, chambers of commerce,
church councils and health councils are examples of
federative organizations where the primary authority
resides in the units that make up the councils.

Because so many different groups have to be con-
sulted before decisions can be approved, a federation
is not the type of organization that can act quickly
when action is demanded. In Model Cities planning,
a number of directives can be expected to be sent
from the federal government which may require fast
decisions. To make such decisions the executive committee will often find itself forced to act without
the official sanction of its constituent members or
forego possible opportunities. While these actions
may be necessary, the present mood of the citizen
groups in the Model Cities areas is such that too
many actions taken without their direct involvement
and sanction may well be the cause of internal tensions within such a federative organization.

Federations can generally come to agreements on
broad policy issues, such as favoring small housing
projects to large ones, or stressing the need for
manpower programs in preference to recreation programs. The members of such a council can usually
come to compromise agreements on such matters as the
size of the council, election procedures, statements
of preamble goals, the role of citizens in the planning process and the general allocation of funds for
various types of functions such as welfare, housing,
or education. The problems begin to arise when specific substantive decisions have to be made.

When resources are quite limited, as in the Model
Cities program, a number of concrete decisions will be

required. The HUD regulations as stated in CDA Letters 1, 2, and 4 call for the spelling out of highly
specific operational plans for program implementation
for each year of planning. This requires that specific answers must be given to a number of questions.
What programs will be implemented? Where will the
program be located? Who will be assisted by the program? How much money is required to operate the program? Who will administer it? What are the sources
of funding? What commitments have been made by the
various funding sources to guarantee such resources?
The way these decisions are made in effect determines
which among the constituent units will benefit and
which will be excluded from the Model Cities planning
and program implementation for that year. Numerous
jobs, organizational status and changes in the established community power structure hinge on such decisions.

No matter how rational the process is for arriv-
ing at programs that may be in the best interests of
the Model Cities residents, in fact, political decisions and and the relative influence of the competing
organizations within the federation will ultimately
determine what is planned. Unlike a unitary organization that has an executive at the top to decide suc
issues, a federation is more or less a society of
peers in which no decision made by the federation itself is binding on its constituent units without thei
consent.

For a federation to survive under such circumstances, either the constituent units must give up a
large amount of its sovereignty to the federation's
central executive committee or else it must engage
in difficult bargaining among the constituent units
to arrive at compromise agreements. In New York City
the great difficulty the residents in the three Model
Cities areas have gone through to select local neighborhood directors does not bode well for their future
ability either to meet the federal guidelines within
the designated period of time or to maintain the viability of their organizational structures during the
planning period. The delicate nature of such structures generally results in their making decisions on

which almost all the members agree. But these decisions seldom bring about the basic changes required to improve services and programs for the poor. While organizations may be willing to make minor accommodations to better serve people, they will not make major changes without a struggle. If such changes are demanded of them by the majority of the federative membership, the organization would likely leave the federation. Most delegates are aware of this possibility so that none are willing to push for any major changes from the status quo. In effect, the basic problems remain untouched by latent understanding among the membership not to "rock the boat." This has generally resulted in such organizations evading their responsibility in tackling the problems fraught with the most conflict. And it is to this very type of problem that residents planning the Model Cities program are mandated to address themselves.

If federations with only one functional area of interest to focus on have a difficult time making basic program changes, then the multi-functional interests of a Model Cities federation will find its problems multiplied to an even greater extent. Not only must such an organization contend itself with the power interests within the Model Cities area, but also with the city-wide public and private agencies that have interests in the area.

Yet, there is a ray of hope that innovative solutions may be forthcoming from such a structure. In large cities such as New York City, the presence of two levels of decision-making structures may prove to be the catalytic agent needed to make a federation work. The neighborhood Model Cities council, a federation of subcommittees and subcommunities in the central Brooklyn area, are united by their opposition to control by New York City's CDA. The CDA, in turn, has challenged the citizens council to develop a feasible Model Cities plan for its area. The city's challenge will serve to reinforce the council's desire for internal unity in order to produce this plan and thus meet this challenge. One aim of such councils is to wrest power away and gain control of resources from the central public and private agencies. Studies have

shown that challenges to the integrity of a federative
structure are a strong motivating factor in overcoming
potential internal divisiveness.

However, in smaller cities where there is only
one Model Cities committee, such a division between
the neighborhood's and the city's interests can lead
to irreconcilable conflicts because there exists no
outside "enemy" against which the competing faction
can unite. The conflicting interests are located
within the same structure. This increases the tension within the structure and makes the development
of a Model Cities plan difficult at best. In Hartford, Connecticut, the political parties competed
with each other for control of the Model Cities citizen structure while in New Haven, Connecticut, the
federal officials had threatened to cut off planning
funds unless the mayor, the board of aldermen, and
the citizens were able to come to an accommodation
with each other.

In spite of these potential inner tensions, federative structures do not represent a viable form of
organization to get things accomplished. However,
policy guidelines first need to be established and
sanctioned by the constituent members. These guidelines can then serve the purpose of enabling the members of the federation to perform a number of useful
functions. The guidelines facilitate:

(1) the equitable distribution of resources
(2) coordination of different programmatic
    subcommunities
(3) the resolution of conflicts among com-
    peting interests.

A federation that comprises most of the community
interests becomes almost impossible to dominate by a
handful of members because of the difficulty of a
leadership group finding issues around which it can
rally the majority support of the membership with its
diverse interests.

A federation can thus move a Model Cities program
forward; but the type of planning it does will tend

to be conservative with few innovations. And it will
take longer to formulate a plan agreeable to the majority of its constituent members than in a unitary
structure.

Coalition

A coalition is a weak form of organization in
which autonomous organizations are convened by mutual
agreement to pursue a common goal. Power resides
completely in the autonomous bodies. None is given
up to the convenor or coordinator. The organizations
in the coalition are peers who agree to carry out specific assignments to accomplish an overall goal.
The Urban Coalition is such an organization whose
members agree individually to assist in training and
securing jobs for the hard-core poor. Such a coalition can work well because its general goal is limited
to a single target area in which the members of the
coalition have some stake and capacity to accomplish
its task.

Community development is another form of coalition
which embraces a wide range of goals. The main difference between a single-purpose coalition and a community development body is that the former stresses
getting the task done and then dissolving the coalition and the latter emphasizes community cohesion
with task accomplishment as an important secondary
goal. However, studies of community development efforts reveal that without substantial success in
achieving key community goals, emphasis on community
cohesion is not enough to hold such coalitional attempts together for very long.

A second factor involved in a coalition is its
tendency to disintegrate rapidly when an effort is
made to shift its emphasis from the first objective
to the second one. The "action system" created to
accomplish the original task is usually too fragile
to accommodate the shift of emphasis.

A special form of structure is the "executive-
centered coalition." In this type private and public
interest groups respond to the leadership of a top

executive, usually a mayor, to achieve a range of
goals. New Haven's Mayor Lee achieved brilliant
initial successes in urban renewal, education, and
anti-poverty programs using this type of coalition.
However, with the loss of his chief strategists to
other cities, the underlying tensions that were held
in abeyance by their presence have recently begun to
surface as the mayor has attempted to shift his successful coalition to work on the comprehensive Model
Cities planning. A manifestation of this coalitional
breakup is shown by its difficulty in agreeing on a
formula of who should have what authority on its City
Demonstration Agency. Because of New Haven's difficulty in agreeing to a formula of the composition of
its CDA, that city in April, 1968, was threatened
with the loss of its Model Cities planning grant.
Though the issue has since been settled, the
"executive-centered coalition" which had worked so
effectively up to that time was in serious danger of
breaking up.

A coalition works best under conditions of crisis
a factor that is present in our urban slums and which
appears to be a motivating force in the Model Cities
program. And it works well when one group feels itself under attack by another. In the Model Cities
areas, the threat of riots is a strong factor in which
both the residents of the poverty areas and those living in the affluent parts of the city feel under potential attack from each other. While both sides are
taking precautions to protect themselves, they have
also managed to take those first tenuous steps necessary to work out Model Cities organizational structures even though they really satisfy no one. While
structurally most of the Model Cities CDAs may be
unitary or federative structures, in spirit they are
really coalitional in nature.

One of the main goals of the Model Cities program
is to bring about a better coordination of services.
A coalitional structure is one way to achieve this.
New York City's Model Cities Committee, for example,
is made up of six city agencies whose members were
appointed by the mayor. Each of the six members has
a veto. Although votes are taken, none of the six

agencies are legally bound by the decisions but rather are morally obligated to live up to the letter of those agreements. The veto is to be used only when a basic policy of any one of the agencies is violated by a majority decision of the other five agencies. The mayor's committee, in effect, represents a coalition in which the efforts of the six agencies are painfully trying to bend their resources and programs into a coordinative attack on the causes of poverty. Thus far this arrangement has been successful because of the cooperative spirit of its members. But more important, the difficult decisions that may affect the operations of their agencies have not had to be faced yet. How it responds under citizen pressures during Model Cities planning will determine how well this structure really works.

The larger the number of autonomous bodies that constitute a coalition, the less likely that it can hold together long enough to achieve even a limited objective. New York City's Model Cities Committee, in recognition of this fact, has deliberately kept its membership to six members. It is devising other methods for communication with other public, private, and neighborhood groups concerned with Model Cities planning. The very tenuousness of a coalition makes it the least likely organizational structure to plan a comprehensive Model Cities program. Because of the large number of diversified self-interest groups that are claiming a role in the Model Cities planning process, such a body has little likelihood of being adopted or working successfully in any municipality of 50,000 or more. It has a greater chance of success in communities where power is held by a relatively few leaders or organizations. This is more apt to happen in small towns than in large cities.

Other Types of Structures

There are two other, looser types of organizational structures that deserve some mention. While it is unlikely either will be adopted by any of the Model Cities cities, they do represent possible ways of organizing communities that reject any type of tight community organization.

Congress of Organizations

A congress of organizations represents an assemblage of many diverse community units. A convenor, usually associated with the Model Cities staff or CDA, will take responsibility for calling such an assembly together. He or his designee will serve as the moderator of the open-ended deliberations that take place. The convenor has no sanction from the assembled members to convene them. Each member of the assembly comes of his own accord and participates as he sees fit. Votes are taken only to get a "sense of the assembled" members' wishes on specific issues. They are not binding on those present but are used to assist the convenor in guiding the Model Cities staff to arrive at planning decisions.

Such a congress offers no continuity in its deliberations. Yet it serves several purposes. It offers a means of communication on a wide variety of issues for the numerous self-interest groups residing in the Model Cities area. It permits the convenor to share information with those assembled. It enables the assembled to offer their own recommendations on many issues. It is a means to ventilate feelings by the assembled. Finally, it provides an informal means for the convenor to gain a sense of the community's feelings toward CDA, its planning efforts and the nature of the community's problems.

If the same members come together often enough so that a spirit of mutual respect and concern for improving the Model Cities area develops, then it is possible for such a congress to convert itself into a more formalized federation or coalition. Such a congress of citizens did in fact lead the assembled to support an urban renewal plan that was developed by the Boston Redevelopment Authority in the Roxbury section of Boston. After the plan was approved the members of the assembled decided to formalize themselves.

There are dangers in using this model for Model Cities planning. Great powers are placed in the hands of the convenor to evaluate the sense of those

assembled when in fact the wide diversity of opinions
expressed on a number of issues permit no one point
of view to dominate. Furthermore, without any formal mechanism for making binding decisions, bitter
controversies and organizational rivalries can so
disrupt such meetings that even the freedom to express ideas openly become curtailed or limited. Such
meetings are an open invitation for any militant
group which disagrees with the whole concept of the
Model Cities program to use power tactics to disrupt
them and prevent an exchange of views. Whereas such
an assembly would have been considered a possible
mechanism for obtaining a "sense of the community"
previous to the creation of the anti-poverty program,
the tensions and strong differences of opinion that
exist in the Model Cities areas today would indicate
that such an informal means for involving citizens
would be rejected by the citizens themselves and by
federal officials. It would not embody the real
spirit of citizen participation reflected in "CDA
Letter No. 3."

Functional Committee

The functional committee is a structure which is
composed of a number of isolated committees called
together by a CDA staff member. Each committee would
be composed of the relevant community leaders and the
associations that are most concerned with their area
of interest, such as education, retardation, health,
manpower, and so forth. The committees would be ad
hoc, have only advisory power, and be disbanded at
the request of the convenor. The CDA convenor would
coordinate the efforts of these several committees.
From their ideas, he and his staff would develop a
series of programs to meet the needs of the people in
the Model Cities areas. Once the convenor has molded
the several committees' programs into a coherent,
comprehensive plan, he would circulate it among the
committees or at a series of open community meetings
to get the people's reactions to the plan. Because
most of the power remains vested in the CDA convenor,
he would have the final power to accept, modify, or
reject the suggestions offered by the community and
the ad hoc committees.

This type of Model Cities planning structure
places maximum responsibility on the CDA. It is extremely time-consuming for a staff to man a number
of different committees at the same time and coordinate their several efforts. The burden of criticism
falls most heavily on the CDA if it fails to develop
a plan that satisfies a wide spectrum of the community's interests. Because the functional committees
do not have final decision-making over what happens
to their proposals, they can criticize the CDA for
not accepting their ideas while gaining credit for
those that are accepted and generally well received
by the community at large. The citizens in this type
of structure would have responsibility without authority.

This is a highly unique type of planning structure. It is doubtful that the federal officials would
accept such an interpretation of citizen involvement
except in very unusual circumstances. On the other
hand, the mood of the citizen leaders in the Model
Cities communities would not accept such half-measures
as being meaningful citizen participation.

CONCLUSION

The unitary structure of citizen organization
that can lead to quickly planned action programs demanded by the residents and federal officials is the
least likely structure to develop because of the numerous self-interest groups that must be involved in
the Model Cities planning and implementation process.
Whether we are talking about small, medium-sized or
large cities, the type of structure that will eventually evolve will be some variation of a federation.
The nature of a federation does not generally produce
either very innovative or quickly planned programs
except in circumstances of crisis, community likemindedness or strong outside pressure to meet timetables. Fortunately, two of these conditions exist:
the crisis within the Model Cities areas to produce
quick, visible signs of change and the pressure from
federal officials to meet their planning deadlines.

Community likemindedness exists only in the sense that the residents are demanding changes in the ways the school, health, welfare, police, and other services are now offered. They differ widely on solutions and on who should be involved in guiding the direction of such proposed changes. Thus, in those program areas where common agreement can take place, it may be possible to expect creative programs to emerge. Otherwise, in the arena of unresolved differences among the numerous self-interest groups, incremental changes or small adaptations to the current programs will be the order of the day.

Regardless of the number of members in the federation, a small executive committee, another planning committee, should be formed to help move the efforts of the larger structure with its subcommittees to points of decision-making. It can be expected in time that the members of the federative structure may relinquish most of its authority to the executive committee. The executive committee would then function informally in the capacity of a board of directors, typical of a unitary organization. If this should occur, the best features of both types of structures, the democratic representation of a federation and the rapid decision-making of a unitary structure, would have evolved.

However, regardless of the structure that evolves, there is no way any structure can guarantee that its programs will be any more creative than those which already exist. The citizen body may well guarantee a better delivery of services; it will undoubtedly result in the expansion of services in the Model Cities neighborhoods; and it will produce a larger and more assertive role for the citizens in setting their own program priorities. If these were the only benefits for the programs, then these gains would bear impressive testimony to the importance of the Model Cities program.

CHAPTER **5** RELATIONSHIP OF CITIZEN
ORGANIZATION TO PUBLIC
AND PRIVATE SECTORS

The last chapter discussed the role and possible
organizational structure of citizen activity; this
one will focus on the relationship between the citizens and a number of other bodies with which they
must work. An assessment will also be made of the
probable influence citizens can have on these various
groups. In order, the discussion will focus on the
following groups: the public sector, local and state,
and the private sector, involving local and national
business groups and voluntary welfare agencies.

PUBLIC SECTOR

The major inputs in the Model Cities areas have
traditionally come from public agencies. The most
obvious public services used by the residents have
been the public schools, welfare assistance, police
protection, sanitation, housing and health services.
More recently, mental health, alcoholic, recreational, manpower and economic development programs have
begun to receive more emphasis under the impact of
federal resources made available in these program
areas. The low-income residents have had more experience with the longer established services and therefore have focused most of their attention on them.

Prior to the advent of the anti-poverty and Model
Cities programs, the voice of the citizen had little
effect in changing the character of these services.
This lack of responsiveness to citizen demands for
change generally resulted in an increasing belliger-
ency on the part of the low-income residents to

these public agencies and their staffs that provide
the services.

There are three forces citizens must contend with
if their actions are to produce any real change. They
must change: the laws, the administrative interpretations of the laws, and the attitudes of the administrators who carry out the regulations.

Most of the current programs are governed by
legislation that determines the functions, scope,
financial resources and goals of the various services.
Congress has been responsible for the creation of most
of the laws whose programs affect the Model Cities
areas. For example, the Social Security Act has set
the pattern of welfare assistance, disability insurance, pension plans and medical services. Some of
these legislative acts have required the passage of
state enabling legislation before the services could
take effect in the local communities. For example,
not all states provide health benefits to public assistance recipients under Title 19 of the Social
Security Act. In other programs such as OEO and Model
Cities, the federal laws permit direct access on the
part of the federal departments to the municipalities
without requiring prior state enabling legislation.
Thus, how the legislation reads has a powerful influence on what services are provided to the local communities. Citizens can alter this legislative intent
only by influencing the legislators responsible for
making such laws. This usually requires national or
state strategies. The unconcerted efforts of residents in the 150 now existing Model Cities areas will
not generally have enough impact to bring about desired change in the law to overcome the conservative
influence of non-urban legislators.

However, as the number of cities in the program
increases and they begin to concert their activities,
it can be expected that their influence will grow.
The Model Cities areas have an opportune moment in
this new Presidential administration to influence the
direction of Nixon's policies toward solving urban
problems. They can best do this by spelling out the
problems resulting from the current programs and

suggesting ways of solving them in their Model Cities plans.

The second force citizens must contend with are the administrative interpretations of the law. Federal legislation is usually broadly written so that different states and administrators have wide latitude in rendering their interpretation of the law's intent. What should be the eligibility criteria for entrance into public housing? Should there be residence requirements which potential recipients must meet before they are eligible for welfare assistance? How long should the waiting period be before a person is eligible for unemployment compensation? How state legislators and administrative officials answer these questions affects thousands of persons and determines their eligibility for public services.

The interpretations given to the laws are usually based on the availability of resources, the attitudes and beliefs of those political and administrative officials who make such decisions, and the administrative capacity of the local agencies to realistically provide the services. For example, these three factors are implicitly taken into account when public officials determine welfare eligibility requirements. The requirements state how much the state or local government can afford, how the general public through its representatives and public officials feels about who should have welfare assistance, and how capable the staffs of welfare departments should be in rendering these services to the eligible recipients.

When residents in the Model Cities areas decide to change the administrative regulations that govern how services are rendered, they must evaluate the strength of the forces that laid the basis for these regulations in the first place. Only if there has been a general shift in these underlying forces can determined citizen action result in meaningful changes. And even when such changes have been made, the complexities of the bureaucratic structure often result in the changes mandated at the top being deflected from their intent as these changes are implemented by the staff members required to carry them

out. The Board of Education of New York City, for
example, has claimed that in response to community
criticism it has made many innovative changes to improve education for those living in the poverty areas.
Yet, studies have shown that seldom have they been
carried out so that they made any difference to the
Model Cities residents.

Fortunately for Model Cities citizen planning,
the trend toward local decision-making and the decentralization of services is consistent with the thrust
that many of them will be advocating. Instead of
creating a new trend, or fighting a firmly entrenched
way of doing things, the citizen planners will be
giving an impetus to a movement that has been under
way for at least five years and gaining momentum.

The third force citizens must contend with to
bring about change in public services is the general
resistance of the directors of these programs to any
changes they perceive as a threat to their power.
Yet, Model Cities planning calls for the coordination
of public programs to make them more responsive to
resident needs. Although the proponents of coordination
state that the new systems of delivering services will
enhance the effectiveness of all programs, the directors fear a loss of control over their individual
programs without a corresponding guarantee that greater effectiveness will follow. They consequently resist becoming too much involved in the coordination
of their programs. The result is that the directors
of public programs can in their own way undermine the
very essence of the intent of the Model Cities legislation. Furthermore, a mark of success of an agency
and its administrator is its ability to expand its
program boundaries on a yearly basis. The more an
agency can extend its jurisdiction over new programs,
the greater its power base becomes. Model Cities
citizen councils, on the other hand, aim to gain control over some of the functions and programs of these
public agencies and thereby limit or reduce their
power base. The fight for decentralization of New
York City's education system has this as one of its
central issues. The same is true in the fields of
economic development, housing, and delivery of health
services.

Yet, there are encouraging signs in New York City, for example, of these agency administrators' recognition of the need to share power with local residents. Administrators, who are more flexible in their capacity to work with local residents, are beginning to replace those who prefer to maintain their power base tightly clutched in their own hands. Success is being measured by a new standard. Producing beneficial results is more important as a measure of success than is citing how a program has grown in size regardless of the kind of results produced.

Thus, the citizen councils have to challenge three powerful forces if they are to change the nature of the public programs which they assert so poorly serve them: the federal, state, and local legislative bodie the administrative interpretations of those laws; and the resistance of the administrators themselves to any threats to their power and right to administer the programs as they see fit.

If the forces arrayed against the citizen councils seem powerful, the citizens in the Model Cities areas have weapons that they can use to combat these forces. First, the Model Cities law itself and the regulations interpreting that law mandate planning and policy-making roles for the citizens. While each Model Citie community will interpret differently the relative role of the citizens and the city administration, HUD and OEO officials are pressing for a strong citizen role in the decision-making process. This means the residents of the Model Cities areas will have much more influence over the public programs that are now operating in their areas than heretofore.

Secondly, the existence of the anti-poverty community action programs has given local citizens a potent force to disrupt services unless they are more responsive to their needs. Sit-ins, picketing, boycotts and even violence in the burning and looting of stores, homes, and public facilities are direct and aggressive tactics residents have used to express their anger at what they consider unresponsive public agencies. Welfare, education, police, and fire protection agencies have been the major targets that have

felt the brunt of such actions in the past few years.
The threat of ever-increasing violence in our urban
centers is no longer taken lightly. The Model Cities
citizen councils can turn this potential for destruc-
tion into a highly constructive force to revitalize
their communities. But this can be done only if the
public agencies and their officials meaningfully involve themselves in the planning process.

The third source of influence the citizens have
is the creation of competitive, parallel institutions.
The Community Action Agencies, financed by anti-
poverty funds, are new agencies that are serving the
poor in competition with the established neighborhood
settlement houses, legal agencies, and social service
agencies. The creation of the Manpower and Career
Development Agency in New York City is another parallel organization that competes with the services offered by the U.S. Employment Service and Board of
Education sponsored training programs. They are competitive agencies because each reaches out to serve
the same clientele. The more effective the newly
created agency is, the more pressure is placed on the
established agency to change its administrative practices or to go out of business.

The Model Cities program requires that both the
public sector and the local residents work out solutions to the community problems. Each side must
therefore make some kind of accommodation to the other.
Otherwise, both suffer. While the children will not
be better educated in a hostile and disruptive atmosphere, neither will the school board be able to carry
on business as usual. Neither will urban renewal and
housing agencies be able to build improved housing
and community facilities unless they can guarantee
local residents more control over the jobs connected
with such construction and the operation and ownership of the housing and community facilities that are
created. In almost every vital program so necessary
to meet the needs of local residents, a stand-off will
take place unless both sides cooperate. An agency
director who believes in extending his power cannot
afford such disruptions for very long without a serious threat to his continuation in office.

In Model Cities, the citizen councils will demand greater control over "new" programs that are started in their areas, such as the concentrated employment program, the community action program, community mental health demonstration programs, vest-pocket housing and recreation programs. This is often made possible because such programs may not be bogged down in the legal or administrative bottleneck that are more likely to inhibit changes in the more established programs such as welfare, education, and police.

However, citizens can expect to have increasing influence in bringing about incremental changes even in the more established programs by serving on advisory boards and increasing their influence in the planning process. Nevertheless, their influence is still constrained by the fact that it is often state and federal legal and administrative procedures that limit the amount of change they can bring about without going through the politics of changing the laws themselves.

With regard to state-financed programs that affect Model Cities residents, such as state mental hospitals, higher state education policies, or mass transit programs, local citizen councils can expect to have little or no creative involvement in the decision-making and planning of these programs. Their main influence is derived from taking stands on projects already or about to be approved, such as the proposed Lower-Mid Manhattan Expressway, or the location of state-sponsored recreation facilities. Demonstrations opposed to such projects may hold them up but it is unlikely that they will prevent their eventual completion. Support for them will speed up their implementation. The reason for their reduced influence on state-operated projects stems from the limited constituency represented by the Model Cities citizen bodies compared to the far larger constituencies not involved in Model Cities planning. Only as Model Cities planners sharply define problems and identify solutions that touch upon similar issues in non-Model Cities neighborhoods will their influence to change state legislation be felt. It is quite likely that MC planners will be more effective in attracting

support around the problems they identify than around
their proposed solutions. It is far more difficult
to achieve a consensus around a solution than in
agreeing on the nature of the problem. The difficulties inherent in finding a consensus around the issue
of school decentralization in New York City is a case
in point.

In summary, then, in the public areas there are
degrees of control the citizen councils can anticipate in the planning and execution of Model Cities
programs. Newly funded programs, demonstration programs and programs funded by Model Cities supplemental
grants will come under their control to the greatest
degree; established public programs such as welfare
to a lesser extent; and state-operated programs to the
least degree.

There are then degrees of control local citizen
groups can have over the established programs. In
order of difficulty, the citizens will find changing
federal and state laws most difficult, administrative
interpretations of the laws less difficult, and local
procedural, personnel and program practices least
difficult.

PRIVATE SECTOR

There are several different types of relationships
to be considered in the private sector--local business, national business, and health and welfare institutions. These will be discussed in turn.

Local Business

Local business consists of private enterprises
that depend for their existence on the markets within
the Model Cities areas. Small grocery stores, dress
shops, specialty stores, drug stores, real estate
offices, restaurants, and so forth are the types of
businesses that fall into this category. Many of
these businesses belong to one or more businessmen's
associations or to a local chamber of commerce. These
bodies in turn are expected to seek and be given

representation on any local Model Cities citizen council. As such, the citizens' council and the local business sector can be expected to influence each other in what programs are planned in the area of economic development. The major confrontation that may take place will be between the locally owned and the absentee owned businesses. The pressure of the local citizen councils will be for ownership of the local ethnic groups. Any economic assistance or funds that are made available will thus tend to benefit resident businessmen in preference to non-resident owners. Because the initiative rests with the citizen bodies in such situations, non-residents can anticipate an increasingly competitive disadvantage in the operation of their businesses.

Outside Business

Outside business consists of city-wide and national firms with sufficient financial assets to permit them to expand into the Model Cities areas. Supermarket chains, branch banks, branches of downtown department stores like Gimbels, Jordan Marsh, or Wanamakers, and subdivisions of large companies like Ford Motors, Bell Telephone System, or Allied Chemical are the types of outside business referred to in this section. In general, citizen councils can expect to exert very little influence over the decisions of whether or not these companies expand into the Model Cities areas. This is so because they have no representation on the boards of these firms, where the decisions are made. The movement of these firms into Model Cities areas will often be dictated more by moral considerations than by economic motivation; they have many alternative sites on which they can locate their branches. But the powers of the citizens over the firm's decision to locate in the poverty areas must necessarily be minimal.

However, once the decision is made to expand into a Model Cities area, the citizens have a number of options open to influence the business pattern of these companies. They can expect to serve on a local advisory board that may be attached to the local branch. This advisory board can assist in making

decisions on problems connected with the implementation, construction, and staffing pattern of the firm.
Some citizen plans may call for a share in the ownership of any business located in the Model Cities area
as well as training programs that will prepare local
residents to take over and operate these businesses
within a few years after their establishment. The
issue that faces the citizens is whether it is more
important for them to make high demands for shared
ownership and management of the business as a condition for its coming into their area with chances of
possible rejection or to welcome the presence of such
business as an economic stabilizing force that can
lead to increased opportunities and opportunities for
minority-owned subsidiary businesses that service the
larger firms. In sum, the bargaining power of a citizen group is weak with respect to outside firms compared with their influence over local businesses.

Health and Welfare Institutions

Health and welfare institutions are those agencies
that concern themselves with remedying the basic
problems that beset families in such fields as health,
family counseling, and social welfare. Settlement
houses, clinics for alcoholics, child care centers,
family counseling clinics, and religious services are
examples of such institutions. Many of the traditional voluntary institutions that have served these poverty areas have either moved away as the population
has undergone shifts from white to black or Puerto
Rican or have been under strong competition from parallel forms of services. Among these are store-front
programs versus traditional individual and family
counseling agencies; community mental health store-
front centers versus traditional child guidance and
adult mental hygiene clinics; Head Start and store-
front academies versus traditional classroom education. As a consequence of this shift in the way
services are rendered to residents in the Model Cities
areas, the traditional institutions have lost much of
their influence with the numerous citizen organizations that have sprung up in the last few years. The
main influence of such established agencies will be
in the functional, planning subcommittees of Model

Cities citizen councils. However, in the community-
wide citizen councils such institutions will have
minimal influence. In New York City, they are not
represented on the city-wide Model Cities committee.
Although they may have some representation in the
councils in the three Model Cities neighborhoods, it
is not enough to strongly influence local decision-
making. The chief role of the established voluntary
agencies has been reduced to serving as technical
consultants to the citizens in the planning of social
programs.

In summary, the Model Cities program will tend
to crystallize and establish a whole new set of relationships between the citizens and the other public
and private community forces. Some of these relation
ships will be quite new and result from the existence
of the Model Cities program, such as those with the
business sector and the coordination of public services in multi-service systems. Citizen relationship
with the traditional voluntary sector are still in
the process of transition. Furthermore, the relative
strength of the citizens council in setting policy
with respect to this wide variety of organizations
will vary. Those most dependent on the local resident
for profit or clientele will tend to be more under the
influence of the citizens than those whose resources,
input constituency, and sanction comes from sources
outside the community such as a welfare department,
mass transit authority, or national firm. The Model
Cities residents' capacity to influence these groups
will also vary from city to city.

ORGANIZATIONAL STRUCTURE AND CONFLICTS

The advent of Model Cities has added a new dimension to the already overburdened effort of New York
City to reduce administrative inefficiency by the
creation of "super-agencies." These combine under
one administrator the functions of a number of other
previously related, but autonomous agencies, commis-
sions, or administrations. The restructuring of these
massive changes has been a monumental task in itself.
The task is still not completed in New York City, with

serious questions being raised by the City Council
of its accepting the biggest of these new administrations, the Human Resources Administration, in its
present organizational form.

The changing of roles, the adding of new centralized and decentralized functions and officials, the
new definition of authority and responsibility among
the previously autonomous agencies, the new political
alliances resulting from the new organizational patterns, and the new programs and administrative practices represent only a few of the more basic changes
that these "super-agencies" will have to work through.
New tensions that arise from such massive organizational changes have an unsettling effect on both officials and their civil service staffs. These changes
have been made to improve efficiency, increase service
to the public, foster greater citizen participation
in anti-poverty programs, and facilitate administrative decisions on personnel, budgeting, and program
matters. During the shakedown period, this attempt
at efficiency may seem to result in even more inefficiency than the previous system, but in the long run
these new administrative systems may well prove themselves.

On top of these changes, a Model Cities program
enters the arena and demands even more changes: the
formation of a Community Demonstration Agency (CDA),
the involvement of the local Model Cities residents,
increased participation by the private business sector, and the encouragement of innovative programs and
systems of delivery. These two vast systems of administrative changes have naturally created even more
conflicts within and between the city agencies. These
tensions can best be grasped by an analysis of the
Model Cities organizational structure.

The structure appears simple enough. The mayor,
the formal chief executive of the CDA, has delegated
his responsibilities to a policy-making board of six
administrative officers. These are the chief executive officers of the City Planning Commission, who
serves as chairman; the Housing and Development Administration (HDA); the Human Resources Administration

(HRA), the New York City Housing Authority; the Bureau of the Budget; and the chairman of the Council Against Poverty. There are no voting representatives on this body from any of the three Model Cities areas of the city. The neighborhood directors of the three areas are active, non-voting participants, who are supposed to represent the interests of the citizens while interpreting the policy and intent of the city to those official bodies. The CDA is administered by an executive secretary, who is responsible for the day-to-day operations of its office of Model Cities.

As noted in a previous chapter, HRA was supposed to be the primary social planner and the Housing and Development Administration (HDA) the primary physical planner for Model Cities. All other city administrative units were to be coordinated by these two administrations for purposes of Model Cities planning. This has meant, for example, that the Health Services Administration, a large city operation in its own right, would have its planning effort directly coordinated by HRA which would represent its interests on the CDA's policy committee. However, it was never made explicit to the city agencies not sitting on the policy committee which would be coordinated by HRA and which by HDA. Is the police department, for example, to be associated with HRA or HDA, or both? This lack of definition has often resulted in these agencies doing pretty much as they please.

The final piece of this structure refers to the neighborhood organizations. Each of the Model Cities neighborhoods was to have its own neighborhood director and planning staff. The director was selected by the mayor from a list of names presented to him by a citizen selection committee. Elected neighborhood policy-making boards were created and had the primary responsibility for planning their own model neighborhoods. The mayor's policy committee agreed to accept whatever plans these neighborhood citizen planning bodies adopted provided they were:

  (1) In compliance with HUD guidelines
  (2) Not illegal

    (3) In conformity with the city's basic
        policies
    (4) Feasible to implement with adequate
        funding

On the surface, it appears that the city was
giving a major share of the planning effort to the
citizens while minimizing its own responsibilities
and authority. The mayor's policy committee reasoned
that if it was delegating so much of its responsibilities and functions to the citizens, then it saw little need to give the citizens a vote on its committee.
The action was really in the neighborhoods rather
than at City Hall. Let us look at this simple structure and note some of the numerous unanswered problems it has created.

First, is the CDA itself a legitimate city administrative unit? Created by an executive order, it
seems to hold all powers to order the city's vast
bureaucracy to march in some sort of coordinative and
cooperative step. Its true role and authority has
never been defined. Therefore, its power seems to
come from the high priority the mayor has given to the
Model Cities program rather than from any state or
federal constitutional, legislative, or administrative
mandate.

Must a city official respond to a request for
cooperation? Considering the issues raised by the
creation of these new "super-structures," which their
administrators are trying to cope with, where do they
place this new demand for coordination on their priority list of tasks to accomplish? Is Model Cities
coordination more important than carrying out the
mandate of their agencies, which cover a much wider
constituency than the three Model Cities areas? If
the programs they must carry out by law are in conflict with the programs being devised by another city
agency, who works these differences out and what is
the process by which it is accomplished? For example,
will the city's Civil Service system make allowances
to permit experienced, but academically deficient,
minority residents to work key positions in Model
Cities-sanctioned programs? Will the Housing Authority

change its eligibility requirements to permit previously ineligible welfare families to enter its
housing units?   It is questions of this type that
come before the CDA.   Except for the commitment of
the Mayor to the program, what other powers does the
CDA have to foster such changes among the different
units of the city bureaucracy?   Some have stated that
the CDA is really legitimated to coordinate and in
that capacity to act as a catalyst to encourage other
city agencies to make the necessary legal, administrative, and policy changes that are required to make
the Model Cities program work.   If it has no real
authority to enforce its coordination function, then
does a CDA represent mere excess administrative bag-
gage for the voters, the citizens, and other agencies
to cope with?   While everyone acknowledges the need
for some agency to play such a coordinative role, is
such coordination possible without the full authority
and power of the Mayor behind it.

Second, within the administrations of the new
super-agencies, there are a number of unresolved ques
tions.   Citing HRA for illustrative purposes only,
who has the responsibility for planning: the five
constituent agencies which make up HRA or its central
office planning arm?   Within HRA, each of its constituent agencies has a manpower component of one kin
or another although the major responsibility falls to
its Manpower and Career Development Agency (MCDA).
The policies, eligibility standards, administrative
practices, intake procedures, and designation of target population differs among the five constituent HRA
agencies.   Is it MCDA or HRA's program planning and
development unit which is the major voice in determining how these manpower units are to be coordinated
in an efficient manner?   If HRA, should MCDA have its
own planning unit and, if so, for what purpose? There
are numerous overlapping target populations, function
and roles among these agencies.   Youth are served by
the welfare agency, the anti-poverty program, the
youth service agency, the manpower agency, and addiction service units of HRA.   Who plans for youth and
on what basis?   As autonomous agencies, each of these
five constituent units have already carved out its
own target population and strives to serve it to justify its continued existence.   Within a super-agency,

the duplication of effort and ambiguities of goals
and functions among the different programs become
much more apparent. Such administrative and policy
overlaps must be resolved. Each agency naturally
fights to maintain its existence and roles and claims
the right to arrogate for itself the functions of the
other units. The battles, while fought out internally, affect what happens in Model Cities planning.
Key city agencies cannot be responsive to the needs
and demands of Model Cities residents if their own
houses are not in order.

The New York City CDA assumes that HRA would take
the major responsibility for organizing the residents
in each model neighborhood to create a local planning
unit. Yet, despite its considerable expertise and
knowledge in this area, HRA is at the same time engaged in its own struggle to create citizen-controlled
community corporations. These local aims of the anti-
poverty program in fact are mandated to carry out many
of the same functions as the neighborhood Model Cities
committees. With its limited manpower, an anti-
poverty agency does not have the resources to organize
both citizen efforts. Even if it did, should it use
its staff to create what it considers a competitive
citizen planning body that duplicates the efforts of
the community corporations? To what extent can the
CDA legitimately rely on this HRA unit for carrying
out functions that go against its own best interests?
What authority does the CDA have to demand this unit's
carrying out this citizen organizing function? Such
questions are never answered in words as they are by
actions or inactions. Meantime, policy decisions are
made by the CDA which vitally affect the interests of
some of the super-agencies and their usual way of
doing things.

Thus, we have demands made upon the super-agencies
to cooperate, coordinate, and change their style of
doing things even before they have had an adequate
period of time to organize their own administrations
into smooth working organizations. For the top officials of these agencies, their priorities are determined by their capacity to produce results in those
functional areas for which they are funded. Every-
thing else is secondary. One of these secondary

priorities is the Model Cities program, which tends
to inhibit rather than expedite the super-agencies'
capacity to move ahead. On the other hand, the CDA's
main priority is to reorganize a large, unwieldy bureaucracy to create a comprehensive plan for the most
needy areas of the city. It is less concerned with
the internal conflicts and tensions within the city
agencies than it is with those agencies' ability to
be flexible enough to respond to the needs of Model
Cities planning. The result in New York City and
elsewhere is often a stand-off with little accomplished because each city agency must first determine
its own priorities.

If these differences within the family of city
agencies were not enough to contend with in Model
Cities planning, the necessity to involve citizens
only adds to the complexities and makes the task
even more difficult. Although the citizens are told
to plan, they are not given the tools, authority, or
technical expertise to carry out this task. In New
York City it is the neighborhood directors who speak
for the citizens. Yet, in two of the three Model
Cities areas the director selected was not the citizens' first choice. Is it any wonder that in those
two areas they are much further behind in the planning process than in the third area where the director was the citizens' first choice? In case of a
disagreement with the director, what rights do the
citizens have to take their case to the mayor's policy
committee? How do they fire their director if they
cannot work with him? Who determines what staff they
will have and what the personnel standards are: the
city or the citizens? Unless they have direct access
to the mayor's policy committee, how will they know
what basic city policies will come into conflict with
proposals they desire? To what extent will the city
agencies be willing to change their programs or methods of delivering services to conform to recommendations proposed by the citizen planners? These are
only a few of the questions that have already been
raised by the citizens in New York's three Model
Cities areas. Answers to these questions have been
phrased only in general, vague terms. While this is
an acceptable strategy for a politician, it is not a

strategy that will engender confidence in the city's
intentions on the part of the citizens.

But there is a further question that has to be
raised by citizen planners. To what extent can citizen planning bodies such as New York City's be legitimate as extra-governmental forces? As long as the
mayor's committee does not define what constitutes
basic city policy, then the citizen planner is no more
than an advisor with some influence, but little authority. As long as the citizen does not have a veto
as do the six members of the mayor's committee, then
he has little power to implement his program goals
if they conflict with the basic interests of a city
official sitting on that committee. As long as the
citizen plans what constitutes such feasibility, then
not only is he planning in the dark, but he has little
power to defend his program against the committee's
veto on these grounds. In sum, the citizen-planner
is really legitimated to propose a series of related
and coordinated programs, but with little or now power
to insure their acceptance by the mayor's committee,
which has seemingly given away its planning responsibilities to the communities without, in fact, surren-
dering any of its high trump cards. The answer to
the question of the citizens' legitimacy to plan is
that they have little legal legitimacy and, in reality,
serve as citizen advisory committees.

In summary, the whole Model Cities planning structure is fraught with serious conflicts within city
agencies, between city agencies and citizen-planning
bodies. In New York City, these conflicts are com-
pounded by the fact that the city is already in the
midst of a mammoth transition to bring greater cen-
tralization over its numerous agencies by the creation
of super-agencies. This transition has created numerous organizational and political problems that must
be worked out before serious consideration can really
be given to Model Cities planning. Furthermore, the
politics of government call for making as few decisions as possible on key, conflict issues in order to
keep the agency's options open and its alternatives
flexible. There is merit in such a political stance
and it fits the peculiarities of American politics.

Yet, this stance conflicts with the citizen-planner's
need to know answers to the key questions posed above
so that they know what they can and cannot do. Otherwise, the citizens cannot obtain answers to what the
city means by such phrases as "financially feasible,"
"basic city policy," and "illegal." There is no way
out of this dilemma given the long list of problems
already cited in a Model Cities planning process that
involves the citizen in a partnership with the city
administration. While the complexities of this
partnership with the city administration. While the
complexities of this partnership are more in evidence
in New York City, the same issues confront every city
involved in Model Cities planning.

REALITIES OF CITIZEN PARTICIPATION

The formation of Model Cities citizens councils
must take into account a number of realistic conditions that will have significant consequences for the
task. Four such factors will now be considered:

(1) Struggle for power
(2) Race relationships
(3) Political involvement
(4) Impact of external issues

Struggle for Power

The most important reality that should be taken
into account is the struggle for power among the
minority groups. This struggle was touched off in
demonstrations to achieve civil rights. It intensi-
fied with the dispensing of millions of dollars of
anti-poverty funds in cities around the country. And
it will be further heightened with the advent of the
Model Cities planning and the formation of the Model
Cities citizen councils.

First the federal government legitimized and encouraged the challenge of minority groups and their
leaders to the established programs by the massive
inputs of anti-poverty funds into the community action program. Although these funds were limited,

they were of sufficient amount to touch off an internal struggle among the indigenous leadership for control. Once established, the community action agencies
began to challenge a wide variety of programs that
had served them for years. In addition, the community
action agencies also competed with the traditional
programs by providing services of their own in such
areas as early education, health, manpower training,
and social services. Finally, the community action
agencies then flexed their political muscles by carrying out voter registration drives and supporting
friendly candidates for various offices.

There were both positive and negative consequences
of the numerous actions taken by these new community-
based agencies. On the positive side, the established
agencies such as health, welfare, and police became
more responsive to their demands. Greater restraint
on the part of the police, more regular schedules in
picking up trash, opening of school buildings for
community use, and efforts by the welfare departments
to reduce the bad effects of the eligibility inves-
tigative process were some of the positive reactions.
Political leaders who formerly avoided appearing in
the "slums" began to make more frequent visits and
promises of assistance to the residents in an effort
to gain their votes. Finally, more city and private
agencies were involving the leaders of the poor to
serve on their boards and assist them in improving
their services. These were some of the gains.

On the other hand, there were negative consequences. There were too few resources to meet the
great needs and expectations of the poor. Too few
could be trained for the jobs available. Administrative, union, civil service, educational and health
problems limited benefits to the "cream of the poor."
The hard core were not touched and this increased
their apathy and alienation from even their own leaders. Landlords preferred abandoning buildings to
paying for costly repairs to meet the code standards.
This further reduced the number of available apartments for the poor while creating health and fire
hazards. Private social agencies preferred moving
their services to other neighborhoods rather than

contend with the aggressive and sometimes hostile demands made upon them to improve their services. This
further reduced the quality and quantity of services
for the poor. City agencies tended to make amelio-
rative and temporary improvements in service in response to direct citizen pressure. Once these
pressures were reduced, it resulted in a return to
the former level of service. This token and temporary response to their demands discouraged the poor
and their leaders.

Finally, the actions of Congress toward the Offi
of Economic Opportunity have raised the serious question of whether this new agency will survive. The
insecurity bred by this agency's questionable future
and the manner in which funds have been dispensed to
local programs have further forced the anti-poverty
community leaders to live in an atmosphere of uncertainty. Programs have been arbitrarily cut off or
reduced; budgeted funds have been shifted from one
program to another with little or no notice; and pay-
rolls have been delayed or held up by the inaction
of Congress and OEO.

All of these factors have contributed to interna
dissension among the anti-poverty leaders. Criticism by federal officials or loss of funds have been
excuses for new local power struggles to break out i
attempts to gain control of the programs. In spite
of the frustrations and insecurity inherent in the
program, it has represented one of the major sources
of power and influence for those in control. In New
York City, for example, this control meant the dis-
bursing of some $60 million and thousands of jobs in
1967. It has offered a way for potential leaders to
gain status and prestige. And for those ethnic leaders who could sustain themselves in power, it meant
that they might eventually be in a position to climb
the political ladder to fame and fortune.

Into this atmosphere of tension, frustrated hope
and uncertainty, the Model Cities program has made
its entrance with the same promises previously mouthe
by the leaders of the anti-poverty program--to revitalize the poverty areas and bring dignity to the

lives of their residents. Yet, the funds allocated
to carry out a far wider spectrum of Model Cities
programs are even smaller than those given to the
anti-poverty program. And like the anti-poverty
program, the Model Cities program may not survive.

Yet, in spite of these realities, the same anti-
poverty leaders are trying to control the local citizen councils that are required to help formulate a
Model Cities plan. HUD and OEO officials have further supported resident participation by asking municipalities awarded first round planning grants to
spell out in specific detail the real role of local
citizens in the planning process. Encouraged anew
by the promise of the program and the actions of federal officials, new militant leaders have challenged
the anti-poverty leaders for control of the program.
This challenge has opened up all the freshly healed
scars resulting from earlier battles over control of
the anti-poverty program.

This struggle for power has serious consequences
for the planning of the Model Cities program. The
most important is that it will prevent any real planning from taking place until the conflict is resolved
and the contestants reach an accommodation. In New
York City, this contest went on a full year before
the three citizen councils could be formed. There
are other consequences to be considered. It will
tend to reduce the amount of cooperation required to
coordinate public and private services. It may well
cause hastily drawn and poorly thought-through plans
to be submitted to Washington to meet federal deadlines. It may force greater reliance on city agencies to plan for the Model Cities areas because of
the citizens' inability to agree among themselves.
And it may cause a further alienation on the part of
the poor themselves from their own leadership as they
witness a greater concern on the part of their leaders for power than for producing the new and expanded
services so vitally needed by the poor.

This then is the first reality--the struggle for
power--and all the consequences, good and bad, that
must be taken into account when talking about citizen
involvement in Model Cities.

Race Relations

The Model Cities program will focus on those sections of the inner cities where minority residents
are in the majority. In most cities, this means
working with blacks, Spanish-speaking residents, and
recent white migrants from rural areas. However,
race relations in the United States usually refers
to the tensions between whites and blacks. This relationship is brought into sharp focus in Model
Cities planning because a partnership between the
black leaders and white-dominated public and private
resources is called for. In the anti-poverty program
this relationship was minimized.

The general atmosphere is one of distrust toward
those in control of public and private programs.
Years of broken or half-fulfilled promises, of unre-
sponsiveness to need, and of exploitation have built
up seeds of doubt and suspicion toward white society'
intentions. Urban renewal was often referred to as
"Negro removal." High educational qualifications
have limited job opportunities to only a small minority of those needing work. Promised social services
by the welfare departments to break the "poverty
cycle" have not been forthcoming and then only on a
very limited basis. Blacks are promised their share
of contracts to build public housing and community
facilities only to discover that administrative regulations, bonding and insurance requirements effective
screen out all except those few who had already overcome these barriers. Thus, broken promises have been
a real barrier to better relationships with the white
power structure.

A second barrier is the tokenism of the new programs to revitalize the slums. A "safe and standard"
home in the relocation process has meant improvement
for some residents but, for most, it has meant being
uprooted to a new, unsafe and decrepit slum apartment
Head Start programs had sufficient funds to help only
a fraction of those who could benefit. Training programs too often led to employment in dead-end jobs,
if any jobs at all. It is this tokenism that blacks
point to and conclude that it is really a form of the

whites' way of manipulating them into "cooling" it.
It is a form of co-optation that the black leaders
will no longer accept.

In the Model Cities program they are testing the
good faith of the white community by demanding either
complete or equal influence in the planning and implementation of new programs. Translated into reality this means they want to own the homes that are
built, to manage and be able to buy shares in the
ownership of businesses developed in their areas, to
determine who will operate the schools, welfare departments and training programs that serve them, and
to decide which social programs they want for their
areas. In New York City, this demand has been partially met by giving complete control over demonstration grants and the "supplemental" Model Cities funds
to three local citizen councils created to plan for
their areas.

However, the real test will come when the minority
citizen councils demand that city, state, and federal
officials find ways to overcome the legalistic, administrative, and attitudinal barriers that have stood
in the way over the years of effectively implementing
programs that might make a real impact in revitalizing
the poverty areas.

Added to this black/white relationship is the
friction recurrently breaking into the open between
the Puerto Ricans and the blacks in those cities such
as New York where the two live side by side. Just as
the blacks accuse the whites of not sharing their
power, so the Puerto Ricans have been making the same
accusations against the blacks in the dispensing of
anti-poverty funds and jobs. The Puerto Ricans claim
the white power structure makes concessions to the
blacks, but not to their people. The blacks have had
one or two members on the Model Cities committee of
New York City, the Puerto Ricans none. In the Puerto
Rican-dominated poverty areas, they have hired blacks
in far greater number than has been the case for
Puerto Ricans in black-dominated programs. They point
to the fact that anti-poverty funds funneled into the
black-dominated Harlem and Bedford Stuyvesant areas

have far exceeded the per capita ratio allocated to
the Puerto Rican-dominated programs in the South
Bronx. These inequities between the two groups have
created ill will that has carried over and retarded
the attempt for many months to form citizen councils
in the Model Cities areas.

Thus, internal conflicts between the races residing in the Model Cities areas have added to the com-
plications already prevalent in the distrust existing
between the minority groups and the white power struc
ture. Model Cities planning must take place in the
reality of these tense circumstances that antedated
the initiation of the program but which will color
all the deliberations that occur in its execution.

Political Involvement

The anti-poverty program started from the premise
that the city's political and administrative structur
had become too rigid to be responsive to the needs of
the low-income residents. The initial community action programs were designed deliberately to give the
greatest authority in the operation of the programs
to the poor. The aims were to create pressures from
the poor to bring about basic changes in the structur
of the established public and voluntary agencies and
to compete with them by creating new programs designe
to better meet the needs of the poor. Both of these
objectives necessarily had to engender hostility by
these agencies against the anti-poverty program.

At the same time, the political leadership especially could not ignore the leaders of these communit
action agencies because new political bases were bein
built up that could challenge the unfriendly politica
leader who depended on the poor for a part or substan
tial number of votes. Yet, the political leaders had
little or no control over these programs. At the same
time, the established political leaders harbored mixe
attitudes toward this new breed of ethnic leadership
that was rising in the slums. They could not alien-
ate them, yet they feared that, in time, they would
have to face a confrontation with them if they were
to remain in power. The only way to maintain their

power was to control these programs. This the Green
Amendment has attempted to do for the beleaguered
political leadership.

A similar kind of political ambivalence has ham-
pered the city departmental administrators from taking public stands for or against the new ethnic
leaders and the programs they control. This was due
to the fact that more and more federal funds were
being allocated through their departments to improve
health, education, manpower and other such services
for the poor. These administrators were then placed
in the position of working with the poor to design
new programs to meet their needs while their leaders
were hammering away at their agencies' administrative
rigidities. The administrators were thus forced to
cooperate with their most vocal critics. The new
leaders were not unaware of these ambivalent attitudes
and exploited them in their efforts to gain greater
influence over city programs that were financed with
federal funds.

The Model Cities moved into this fluid situation
and sought to create a new balance of real partnership between the leaders of the poor and the city's
political and administrative leaders. In effect,
the Model Cities program gives the mayor and his department heads more power over the activities of the
poor without necessarily guaranteeing that the poor
will benefit from this new partnership. This is one of
the reasons the poor are demanding that they have at
least an equal if not a dominant voice in Model Cities
planning to insure that any plans and programs they
recommend are not co-opted or sidetracked by the political and administrative power structure.

In New York City, after much deliberation, the
Model Cities committee recognized that they could
not control the leadership of the poor. Furthermore,
it well understood the many divisive forces operating
within the Model Cities areas. Consequently, to min-
imize ethnic pressure against the political and administrative structure, the city encouraged each
Model Cities area to organize itself in its own way.
The citizens felt that the new round of conflicts

they had to endure to create a citizens council was
worth it because they were promised the freedom to
spend the Model Cities supplemental grant as they
saw fit. Only minimal conditions were attached to
this decision. The programs planned were to be accepted provided they were legal, met federal regulations, and were not inconsistent with basic city
policy.

The first reaction to this decision was a positiv
one as it indicated that the mayor and New York City
were going to keep their promise in letting the citizens plan their own programs. It is this consistent
position on the part of the mayor to share more and
more of the planning decisions with the community tha
has sustained his continued popularity among the poor
In the worst riots he has been able to walk unmoleste
and protected by the poor among the rioters.

At the same time, the administrative officials
have not been able to deliver the visible programs
promised and planned by the poor to complete the may-
or's promise. Red tape, bureaucratic inertia, buck-
passing, and administrative rivalry are a few of the
hindrances that have kept the promises from being
fulfilled. The citizen leaders no longer accept such
excuses and will hold the mayor responsible if his
administrators fail to produce tangible results.

One of the consequences of this political and
administrative necessity to produce quick results is
to alter the kind of feasible planning encouraged by
the Model Cities Act. Short-term programs will get
priority over long-term ones. Ad hoc, uncoordinated
planning will take the place of the more tedious,
time-consuming, comprehensive planning. Adaptations
of current programs will gain precedence over innovative ideas. The necessity to produce a politically
feasible plan that can be administered within the
current administrative regulations and structures wil
tend to vitiate the intent of the Model Cities progra
And the pressure to produce such a plan will come as
much from the constituents of the ethnic leadership
as that of the mayor and his administrators in order
to produce quick results.

Thus, while the Model Cities program in New York City has temporarily produced a better balance among the political, institutional, and citizen leadership, the proof of the workability of that balance will show itself only as visible signs of the revitalization of the slums begin to show. The political careers of many people will depend upon that visible evidence of progress taking place soon. And if this does occur, the poor, drawn by the Model Cities program into a new position of shared leadership with the power structure, may well give up their negativistic and distrustful attitudes toward the community and feel themselves an integral part of the city. But the reality of the situation is that the political and administrative power vases start from a defensive position in trying to prove their case to the new ethnic leadership.

External Realities

What happens on the national and international scene strongly shapes the attitude of the citizens toward the type of role they will play in the Model Cities program. Many of the same leaders involved in the anti-poverty programs will also be active in the Model Cities program. They have watched a conservative Congress play a "Perils of Pauline" fiscal drama with their OEO programs. They have watched Congress scale down a rent supplement program as well as funds requested for Model Cities. At the same time, they have seen this same conservative Congress give consent to spending billions of dollars for the war in Vietnam and for the space program. Unable to balance the discrepancy between these two types of expenditures, the ethnic leaders conclude that Congress really does not mean to rebuild the slums.

In New York City, they have observed a conservative state legislature make a sharp cutback in Medicaid funds, reduce construction funds for a major new office building in Central Harlem, and haggle over whether the state has the right to impose its $6 billion building program in the cities. They are the passive witnesses to the large decisions that others make. Yet, they are the ones most vitally affected.

The consequence of this feeling of alienation from the centers of power is to harden the citizen leaders against the local power structure and to make demands to test its sincerity. And at times they claim to see demons where none really exist because they have seen so many in the past that turned out to be very real. The assassinations of Martin Luther King and Robert Kennedy have placed an even greater burden on the white community to prove that Model Cities planning can take place in a peaceful arena rather than in a burning holocaust that threatens all of society.

In summary, the reality factors described in this section will play a powerful part in determining the motivations and attitudes on the part of the ethnic citizen leaders toward each other and toward the po-litical, institutional, and civic power structures that collectively control their destiny. There have been forces at work that have given some credibility to the desire to build a real partnership between the poor and those in power to produce Model Cities neigh-borhoods. At the same time, the strong trend to main-tain the status quo and the failure to offer enough resources to make the whole difficult effort worth-while are obstacles that impede the attempt to create a significant citizen role in Model Cities planning.

Citizen activity is complex and difficult enough as the early sections of this chapter have shown with-out having to take into account the factors discussed above. Yet, important as the results of a Model Citie program may be, the involvement of the citizens in shaping that program is central to the efforts. And because it is central, it is important to shed as much light on the true nature of this much discussed but little understood concept--citizen participation, the life blood of the Model Cities program.

CHAPTER **6** DEVELOPING
A WORKABLE
PROGRAM

THE PRODUCT OF PLANNING

In general, we accepted the notion that planning
is an ongoing process concerned with detailing the
differences between a set of needs and the resources
available to meet these needs. As the mix of needs
and the mix of resources available to meet these
needs change, the plan for meeting this deficiency
must also change. In something as large and as complex as a Model Cities program, it is obvious that
not all unfilled needs will be met; indeed that new
needs will develop as the program progresses, and
that the constant evolution of these needs demands
an ongoing and continual planning process. At the
same time, however, the notion of planning as a process can be overstated because a plan must, at times,
be regarded as the direct and final output or product
of the planning process. To state that planning is
solely a process is to assume that all problems and
all solutions are continuously changing and that there
is no ultimate solution to any one problem. Conversely, to say that the product set by a plan is unchange-
able is similarly incorrect. As needs change, so
must the product of the planning process.

In order to avoid the trap between too fixed a
commitment either to planning as a process or as a
product as the sole rationale for planning, we accepted as reasonable a projected analogue between the
decision-making process and the planning process. We
accepted the concept put forward by Simon and others
on the hierarchy of decisions: the strategic or
value-oriented decision at the top level, and the

fact-oriented decision at the bottom level. According to the model, these lower-level decisions flow
from the earlier prescriptions of policy, which are,
in essence, statements of organizational values. In
the typical business firm, the strategic decision is
regarded as involving a policy decision on the market
that the firm proposes to service, and the product
that it intends to provide that market--or, in other
words, the why of resource allocation. In our opinion, this set of decisions can best be encapsulated
by the proverbial question, "What business are we
really in?"

Because the strategic decision is concerned with
statements of policy on supply-demand relationships,
the notion of its value orientation applies equally
well, although with some modification, to any organization concerned with the delivery of a product or
a service. For example, a city government is con-
stantly faced with a series of value decisions on the
market that it will serve, and the nature or content
of the product that it will provide this market. Although we typically fail to perceive it in this
straightforward a manner, the product of a city is
the range of services--roads, police protection,
schooling, welfare services--that it must provide to
its consumers as compensation for the taxes that they
are required to pay. The decision on what services
the city will provide, the scope and content of these
services, and to whom these services will be provided
is inevitably the outcome of a series of decisions
concerned with social values or political values as
a subset of social values. In both the industrial
firm and the governmental unit, the need for a value
judgment is made necessary because of the proverbial
scarcity of resources, the "why" that we referred to
earlier. All services cannot be provided to all consumers because there is not enough money available to
fulfill all observable needs. Because of this scarcity of resources (and this lack applies to manpower
as well as to money), compromise must be reached and
alternative courses of action selected. This selection of alternative courses of action represents a
compromise. The compromise, in turn, is made necessary by the need to avoid too stark a confrontation

between conflicting value judgments or priorities in
which one subset of needs wins a larger allocation
of resources or an earlier claim to these resources
than another subset of problems does.* Sub-
optimization then occurs. Fewer resources than are
necessary to the complete solution of a problem are
allocated to the problem. Some funds are diverted
to other needs. Some funds are kept in reserve for
contingencies. But no individual problem is granted
its full need for resources except where the problem
can be defined very narrowly, or the need for resources is minimal.

Having made the value judgment on the market relationships that will be developed, an organization
must then determine the optimal mode for the production and the delivery of the services or products
that it has decided to produce. At this point in the
decision-making process the decisions that must be
made are fact-oriented because they are concerned
with the development and implementation of a previously prescribed policy statement.

In theory, there is a best technique for producing
a product and a best method for delivering that product to a most desired group of consumers. At this
point in the decision-making process, the decision-
maker need only be concerned with gathering and an-
alyzing the data that he needs for making appropriate
decisions about the production and delivery process,
since the value or policy decisions have already been
made for him.

In a real world situation, of course, it may be
virtually impossible for the decision-maker to gather
all of the data needed for a truly fact-oriented decision. He may have to rely upon his own intuition

---

*This conflict need not be rational; it can be
motivated by the desire of one group not to be out-
done by another, by non-rational politics (leanings),
or there may be no compromise if the citizen group
elects to put all of its resources into one program
and none into another.

or best judgment in the final selection of the optimal technique available to him for accomplishing his
predetermined goals. Because of the need for personal judgment, even the most factual of decisions
is tinged with subjective value judgments. But this
is the nature of the decision-making process and not
the content of the decision itself. The decision
itself is fact-oriented, it is only part of the process that is value-oriented or subjective in content.
The decision-maker must weigh the cost of perfect
knowledge (if it is available) and the benefits produced by this perfect information. To the extent
that the decision-maker must choose between the cost
of perfect information and the cost of an error in
the decision-making process created by a reliance
upon his own intuition, he is faced with a variant
of a value judgment. But, because of their technological bias, the decisions surrounding the production and delivery system are basically fact-oriented.

Given this model, organizational planning is a
value-oriented process when the prime concern of the
planning is with the selection, over time, of an as
yet undetermined product or service for an equally
undetermined market or set of consumers; in other
words, planning is a process when the decisions to
be made are value-oriented or strategic decisions.
As the market for the product changes--a number of
consumers have been served and are no longer in need
of the product--new decisions must be made on prospective changes in the product line or in the content
of the market that will be served. As long as the
supply-demand relationship continues to change, planning is a process directly related to a value-oriented
decision-making process.

When the problem and solution, if only by definition of the decision-maker, is established, the problem then becomes one of program implementation. At
this level of analysis or action, the output of the
planning process is then a product, i.e., a specific
tangible plan for dealing with a specific problem.
This is the time for decisions on the mode of the
production and the delivery system. Because these
decisions are of a "fish or cut bait" nature, they

are output- or product-oriented. A refusal to commit the output of the planning process to an observable product must at this point in the total planning and decision-making process be regarded as a failure either in the planning process itself or in the administrative process of which the planning process is but one part.

The Project or Program Plan Outline

Despite the value-fact dichotomy discussed above, the development of a project or program plan differs only in scope from the general planning process. Twelve steps must be followed regardless of the level of decision-making: fact or value. In addition, a number of subsidiary steps must also be taken, once again regardless of the level of the decision to be made. The key difference between the general planning process and the project planning phase is in the specificity of the data gathered, and the specificity in the statement of relationships that must be developed. In order to illustrate the greater specificity in project or program planning vis-à-vis the selection of policy and alternatives, an outline of the steps that we regard as essential to both levels of planning is presented. A case history of an economic development program is then presented as an illustration of the use of these twelve steps in project planning.

The twelve steps are outlined as follows:

I. NATURE OF PROBLEM

    A. Definitions
        1. General
        2. Middle-range
        3. Specific

    B. Locus of Problem
        1. Federal level
        2. State level
        3. Local level

    C. Type of Problem
        1. Substantive (program)
        2. Procedural (administrative-legal)

D. Relationships of Problem (as defined)
to other Problems

II. <u>CAUSES OF PROBLEM</u>

A. Discussion of possible theories of
causation from two perspectives
1. Whether cause is <u>unique</u> to Model
Cities area or <u>common</u> to wide
sections of country
2. Whether related to one or more of
the following factors:
a. Economic
b. Social
c. Political
d. Legal
e. Cultural
f. Ideological
g. Technological

III. <u>DATA NEEDED TO PLAN</u>

A. Types of Data Needed
1. Demographic
a. General data
b. Specific data
2. Programmatic
a. General
b. Specific
3. Availability of data
4. Costs to obtain new data

B. Interpretation of Data
1. To explain degree of problem
2. To uncover new problems
3. To relate problems of each other
4. To define possible goals
5. To identify gaps in knowledge
6. To describe extent of existing
resources in quantitative and
qualitative terms

IV. <u>STATEMENT OF GOALS AND APPROACHES</u>

A. Statement of general goals (tells what
concerns community)

1. Within function problem areas,
    state range of goals desired
2. Relate goals to problem and theory
    of causation
3. State goals in quantitative or
    qualitative terms
4. Rank goals on basis of value judg-
    ments and knowledge revealed by
    interpretation of data

B. Identify Alternative Program Approaches
    (tells how goal is to be achieved)
    1. State alternative ways of looking
        at goals in terms of criteria de-
        veloped by community and staff
        Examples of such criteria might be:
        a. Local residents run programs
        b. Fund only programs related to
            economic or job opportunities
        c. First priority given to exist-
            ing programs not currently
            located in the community as a
            health clinic or job training
            center
    2. Rank program approaches on basis
        of value judgments and feasibility
        to execute as related to roadblocks
        that may prevent implementation

V. WITHIN EACH PROGRAM APPROACH STATE TYPE OF
    PROJECTS OR ACTIONS DESIRED

    A. Types of substantive projects
        1. New programs never tried before
        2. Extension of existing programs
            into Model Cities neighborhoods
        3. Improving quality and service of
            current programs

    B. Types of procedural actions desired to
        change any of the following:
        1. Administrative practices
        2. Laws or their interpretations
        3. Service patterns to clients
        4. Staffing patterns
        5. Funding patterns

    C. Rank projects on basis of
1. Cost-benefit analysis
2. Time required to achieve goal
3. Dependence of one project on another

VI. IMPLEMENTATION FACTORS THAT EXPEDITE OR RETARD PROJECT EXECUTION

    A. Types of factors to consider
1. Site location and best use of site
2. Size of program
3. Staffing pattern
4. Training and recruiting of local residents
5. Coordination of program components to each other
6. Flow of administrative authority

VII. COST AND BENEFIT ANALYSIS

    A. Costs
1. Types of cost to analyze in quantitative and qualitative terms
    a. What it costs in dollars, staff, and time to achieve a goal
    b. What resources will be diverted from other projects and costs in terms of this diversion
    c. What it costs if nothing is done about problem (opportunity cost)

    B. Benefits
1. Types of benefits to consider in qualitative and quantitative term
    a. Who will benefit?
    b. How many will benefit?
    c. How will they benefit?
       (1) Short term, (2) Long term
    d. What other programs will benefit by achievement of goal?

VIII. FUNDING OF PROGRAMS

    A. Factors to consider

      1. Cite funding sources
      2. Cite timetable required to obtain
         funds from different sources
      3. Cite constraints on use of funds
      4. If a project requires multiple fund-
         ing sources, how will the timetables
         and constraints be coordinated?

  B. Types of funding
      1. Permanent, recurring expense funds
      2. Capital funds
      3. Seed funds
      4. Temporary or demonstration funds
      5. Reimbursable funds
      6. Revolving funds

IX. STRATEGY FOR ACHIEVING GOALS

  A. Types of strategies
      1. Collaborative
         a. Types of tactics
           (1) Persuasion
           (2) Education
           (3) Exchanging favors
      2. Conflict
         a. Types of tactics
           (1) Demonstrations
           (2) Outvoting opponent
           (3) Violence

  B. Level at which strategy will be used
      1. Local, State, National
      2. Within an organization
         a. Staff
         b. Middle management
         c. Executive
         d. Policy-makers as boards

  C. Resources needed to employ strategy
      1. Manpower
      2. Knowledge
      3. Political strength
      4. Funds
      5. Friendship ties
      6. Time and energy

X.   TIMETABLE

    A.   Expected implementation time period
       1.   Short run: 1st year
       2.   Long run: 2-5 years

    B.   Spacing of projects by years

    C.   Nature of project
       1.   Temporary facility or program
       2.   Permanent

    D.   Relate actions needed to time re-
       quired to gain formal approval for
       project

XI.   MEASURING ANTICIPATED RESULTS

    A.   Quantitative (how many served)
       1.   Ways of measuring
          a.   Total units produced of
             finished product
          b.   Cost per unit served or bene-
             fitted
          c.   Ratio of successes to failures
          d.   Comparison to known city or
             metropolitan average standards
          e.   If an ancillary program (as
             computer center), measure in-
             creased effect on primary pro-
             gram

    B.   Qualitative (how well people served)
       1.   Use of descriptive reports or
          theoretical constructs or ideas
          to measure changes in
          a.   Individual or group behavior
             or attitudes
          b.   Community improvement as
             safety, cleanliness, or in-
            creased pride

XII.   EVALUATION PROCEDURES

    A.   In quantitative or qualitative terms,
       state results anticipated of project.

1. Identify key points in program that
   may determine its success or failure. Among these are
   a. Training of personnel
   b. Administration of program
   c. Coordination
       (1) Between components of same
           agency
       (2) Between two different agen-
           cies
   d. Recruitment of qualified tech-
       nicians or professionals to run
       program
   e. Lack of knowledge to carry out
       program

2. Use evaluation to identify strengths
   of programs and weaknesses to be improved. These lead to

B. Recommendations for change in
   1. Goals
   2. Program approach
   3. Project
   4. Structure of organization

PROLOGUE: ECONOMIC DEVELOPMENT

It was decided rather early in New York City that
economic development could be the cornerstone for any
human-resources-oriented Model Cities concept provided, of course, that the target population ratified
this presumption. The projected emphasis on economic
development grew out of a number of simple concepts
or statements of understanding that the planning
group regarded as a reasonably self-evident expression of American value judgments. From the point of
view of the policy makers with HRA, the breaking of
the so-called "cycle of poverty" by basically economic means was regarded as the underlying goal or
mission of any anti-poverty effort. Given this model, the hoped-for output to be created by this goal
or mission was to be people capable of earning an
income sufficient for their needs, and an income suf-
fient to motivate them to enter into the mainstream

of American life. If this could be accomplished, the
program would be a resounding success. If this goal
cannot be accomplished, however, then any program
dealing with human resource problems will have failed,
regardless of other desirable secondary effects.

Although we regarded this goal as applicable to
all Model Cities and anti-poverty efforts, we felt
that the issue of economic development was manifestly
more critical to New York City (and other very large
core cities, especially those on the Eastern seaboard)
than to many another city or anti-poverty program.
First, New York City is vast in size and complexity:
Merely getting in or out of the city can be a major
task. New industry located in the suburbs--or even
other parts of the city--may be impossible to reach
by either public or private transportation. In some
areas of the city, public transportation is almost
non-existent. In other areas, commuting time between
home and job may be so ridiculously long as to dis-
courage the job applicant. For the most part, the
unemployed or under-employed also lack private means
of transportation to compensate for the lack of public
means. If the large core city cannot be redeveloped,
the ghetto-bound within the city are virtually con-
demned to life-long poverty.

Second, New York City is one of the largest industrial areas in the United States. Within the city
limits, there were in 1967 more than 800,000 industrial employees. However, the total number of manufacturing jobs in the city had been declining for a
great number of years. Some of the loss in industrial
jobs had, of course, been replaced by the growth in
other work classifications: clerical, administrative,
professional, and the service industries, just to
name a few. For the most part, however, these newer
job classifications required the type of skills not
normally possessed by the unemployed or under-
employed. In 1967, according to the Burstein report,
there were an estimated 250,000 unemployed persons
living within the New York City limits. This same
report similarly estimated that there were at least
250,000 unfilled job vacancies in the city. This inability to match the unemployed to available jobs is

due primarily to the unemployed's lack of work skills
although other factors obviously enter into the creation and maintenance of this supply-demand disparity.
We wanted to make an initial effort at finding a way
to match at least some of the unemployed to some of
the available jobs. It was our feeling that if an
economic development program could succeed in New
York, it could succeed in any other major core city!

    Third, we also felt that the critical short-term
need in New York City was the provision of as many
long-term jobs to the unskilled and semi-skilled as
could be made available. This resulted from our assumption that any job created a sense of independence
and belonging that was better than none; that everyone should have the opportunity to gain that feeling
of self-confidence in himself and reasonable trust in
the society around him that an adequate income encourages. Although we recognized the critical need to
upgrade the skills of the existing labor force to better meet the needs of the emerging skills-oriented
labor market, we also recognized the short-term impossibility of that task. Manpower training programs
designed to create a reasonably skilled worker can
cost from $2,000 to $3,000 per person. With 250,000
unemployed in the city, the cost of a massive retrain-
ing program could be as much as $500 million to $800
million. Not only is this sum of money not available,
but there is also an acute shortage of people able to
plan and successfully implement programs of this type.

    Fourth, even if it were possible to budget $500
million to $800 million, and even if it were possible
to find the personnel capable of properly utilizing
this money, the total manpower problem of the city
would still be far from solved. Normal additions to
the labor force among the youth of the city and the
in-migration of unskilled workers from other areas
of the country will continue to generate additional
numbers of unskilled workers in the city for whom
entry-level jobs must be available. A viable industrial base that can routinely absorb some of this unskilled labor is essential if the city is ever to be
relieved of a necessary, but nonetheless oppressive,
social cost. Industry is accustomed to paying for

training needed personnel. Although real, the cost
is generally hidden away in an adaptive cost or price
structure. Because of this, industry can more easily
absorb manpower training costs than can local government. Thus, the real impetus for an economic revival
in New York City must come from the private sector.

Our recognition of the need for a long-term supply of unskilled jobs raised the hackles of many of
our social work colleagues. Their perspective of
the type of jobs that should be provided to the unemployed are those that guarantee a minimum starting
wage of about $100 per week and provide a definite
and obvious career ladder upwards from that initial
starting salary. In addition, they wanted only those
jobs for the unemployed in which the working conditions were "good" and where the job presented what
must, at best, be termed a "challenge" to the individual. They failed to see--or so they stated--the social and economic efficacy of a "dead end" job--or a
job where there was no challenge to the individual's
potential capabilities.

In general, we refuted this view of the world of
work as being invalid although not without many agon-
izing arguments. We maintained, admittedly with much
hyperbole, that most jobs were "dirty"; that most
work environments were somewhat "degrading"; that the
ethic of industry was authoritarian; and that the
notion of social and economic mobility in the United
States--an average industrial wage of $7,000 per
year--was more myth than reality. We also maintained
that most Americans accommodated themselves, if only
unwillingly, to this stark reality. Because of this,
we also maintained that the under-employed and the
unemployed, and the people who try to counsel them,
must face up to the stark realities of the world of
work by plunging into it, and then trying to upgrade
themselves by supplementary education, on-the-job
training, sheer hard work, and other devices that are
or may be available to them. We never quite succeed-
ed in convincing our colleagues of the total reality
of our position, but we did successfully open the
issue for them of the options actually open to the
unemployed and the under-employed. We also raised the

issue of the true capabilities of many of the members
of the target group of the anti-poverty effort and
the fact that a tremendous amount of remedial work
would have to be done with them and for them before
they were legitimately able to expect access to jobs
"with challenges and futures." This remedial effort
will take years.*

This point of view, in turn, raised the issue of
the expectations of the poor. We recognized that the
sudden profusion of community action programs appeared
to promise them quite a bit, but that little substance
has been delivered to them. We recognized that they
had some right to feel alienated from the mainstream
of society and hence suspicious of the alternatives
ostensibly offered to them. In addition, we at Model
Cities had to recognize the validity of their point
of view. Why take a dead-end job that no one else
wants? It doesn't really grant one the sense of self-
confidence or esteem that earning a living is supposed
to do! Nonetheless, we held to our position on the
nature of the jobs that we were most apt to be readily available as being the most realistic and, hence,
in this context, valid.

We also held to our point of view because of our
belief that the core city will continue to be the
point of immigration into an industrialized America
for at least two to three more generations of black
Americans and Spanish-speaking persons (other than
Puerto Ricans) so that our notion on the need for jobs
for the unskilled will, indeed, be a long-term reality. Based upon available evidence, it is now believed that immigrants from rural America and South

---

*The view is held by some that black ownership
of business will make the realities of dead-end jobs
or difficult working conditions more palatable to the
black employee and that the instance of black ownership may help to reduce the present reluctance to accept otherwise dead-end jobs. Only time will tell on
this one. The authors split on the reality of this
situation.

America will have to be accommodated into our society for at least the next fifty to sixty years. Although the provision of jobs for the unskilled laborer may seem brutally exploitative in a modern society, it is nonetheless a dull reality. We wanted to plan for this reality as best we could, and by planning for it, reap some social benefit from the process!

These statements should not, of course, be interpreted as a rejection of the very apparent need for upgrading the skills of the worker so that he can aspire to a job "with a future." Nor should these statements be interpreted as a ratification of any notion that suggests that the core city be the economic home for the unskilled laborer. Rather, we recognized what we felt were the realities of the situation: the continuing in-migration of the untrained into the core city, and the need to accommodate just as quickly as possible these people into the economic fabric of the city. To the extent that a reasonably self-sufficient person can accommodate himself to the society around him, the public sector is relieved of the burden so that it can then devote its limited financial resources to other pressing social problems.

Last, the prognosis provided for the New York City by Vernon, Hoover, and others is that the reindustrialization of the core city, especially one as large and complex as New York, is impossible. These economists maintain that the nature of the core city is such as to make industrial redevelopment impossible. Land costs are high; construction costs are high; logistical difficulties--crowded highways, limited rail access, substandard or non-existent public transportation--all add to the confusion. In shoft, according to Vernon and others, the core city is no longer an economically viable area except for a highly skilled or clerically oriented labor force. The facts available to us also strongly suggested that the industrial base of New York City would eventually wither away, leaving few, if any, opportunities in the city for the unskilled laborer.

The reality of this situation is evident in the statistics available on New York City. However, those

of us responsible for the Model Cities planning process felt that we could not accept this prognosis.
We could not accept it because, if we did, it would
mean that much of the Model Cities legislation and
the anti-poverty effort was irrelevant to the needs
of the real world. Why rebuild housing in Harlem if
the person living in Harlem does not and cannot have
access to an entry-level job? Better, in that case,
to build a one-way road out of the city into those
areas in which jobs do exist! If jobs, and the potential entry into society that they provide, are not
available, the overwhelming thrust of any anti-poverty
effort should then be built on the transmission-belt
notion: Give the person just enough in social services
to allow him to quickly escape the ghetto. And as he
escapes, rip down the buildings that he has left behind so that he cannot return.

Clearly, this is an unacceptable and unrealistic
point of view. Some of the deprived will manage to
escape the ghetto solely on the basis of their own
ability. There are always those who become upwardly
mobile with but a minimum of outside help. However,
most ghetto residents lack the ability to accomplish
this by themselves. They have been deprived and de-
nied for too long a period of time, and too intensive-
ly, for simple remedial measures to be effective.
They are in the ghetto now and they are destined to
remain there for quite some time in the future. If
they cannot be brought into the outside world, the
outside world will have to brought to them. Because
of this, we felt that we had to take a positive attitude toward economic development and pressure that
something could be accomplished. Despite the overwhelming evidence "proving" the impossibility of core-
city economic development programs, we decided to take
a crack at the problem and see what developed.

Our first suggestion for a core-city economic
redevelopment project called for an industrial park
to be located in the ghetto. We hoped that it might
be possible to put together sufficient land area to
provide a manufacturing site for a well-financed,
large-scale national manufacturing corporation. By
doing so, we hoped to accomplish the following:

(1) Provide jobs at the entry level and above
for a substantial number of ghetto residents in a large, prestigious firm.

(2) By using the financial strength of a
large national corporation as the basis
for financing the industrial park, provide new and improved manufacturing space
to a number of existing small manufacturing firms. By doing this, we hoped to cut
down on the out-migration from the city
of the small manufacturing firm which,
typically, is the backbone of the core-
city industrial complex. By slowing down
the out-migration, we hoped to at least
stabilize the job market within the core
city.

(3) By linking city-sponsored manpower training
and education programs to the large firms
and collectively to a number of smaller
firms, provide an incentive to the employer
that might induce him to provide some form
of career ladder opportunity to the ghetto
resident that he would not otherwise provide. The assumption that we made here
was twofold:

   (a) that a large-scale manufacturing operation would, because of its size,
provide reasonably automatic career
ladder opportunities for the ghetto
residents provided only that they were
qualified; and

   (b) that the newly located small firm
would be sufficiently dynamic to grow
in size and, in growing, first create
new jobs and later create jobs that
would demand a more highly skilled
employee.

Once again, we presumed that the ghetto resident,
if he were properly trained, would have first crack
at these newly created opportunities.

THE PLANNING FORMAT: THE NATURE
OF THE PROBLEM

Our earlier discussions on the need for an economic development package within a total Model Cities
program and our tentative prescription of project
content for this package served to define some of the
problems with which we wanted to deal. To the extent
that we could document the reality of these problems
and indicate the practicality of dealing with them,
we could potentially influence the goals to be set
by the Mayor's Committee for the New York Model Cities
program. We knew that the nature of the problem that
interested us would also appeal to them, and for all
the obvious reasons that we have already cited. Indeed, the odds were strongly in favor of this being
their highest priority because of its political visibility, the possibility of a joint private sector--
public sector effort, and the immediate return to the
city that such a program would provide. Despite this
basic appeal, however, the need to more rigidly define
the problem and more accurately assess its feasibility existed. Unemployment and economic development
projects are too broad a classification of need. Specificity in a statement of the problem, project goals,
and task is needed for successful project design.
Because of this, we then began narrowing down our
definition of the problem, and the organizational
goals and tasks prescribed by this narrower description of needs.

The general problem, as we defined it, became the
need for ghetto-based capital formation. The more
specific problem then became the lack of jobs for
ghetto residents. From this came the most specific
definition of the problem with which we wanted to
deal as the need to "stimulate ghetto-oriented capital formation in order to provide long-term, entry-
level industrial jobs for unemployed males, ages
17-26, presently residing in the designated Model
Cities area." Thus, our ultimate goal became the
creation of jobs for these individuals.

Our task, arrived at after a great deal of investigation, was the creation of capital by the provision

of adequate and well-financed manufacturing facilities to small and medium-sized industrial firms with
an observable growth potential. The by-product of
this growth would be the entry-level jobs that we
desired. There are, of course, alternative courses
of action available to the planner given the primary
goal of capital formation and the secondary goal of
entry-level industrial jobs. Black ownership of
ghetto-based business is one example of an alternative course of action, and the alternative most
appealing to the ghetto resident. We did not reject
this course of action nor did we reject the idea of
large-scale industrial parks. We similarly realized
that skills training programs, on-the-job training
programs, similar-type programs are valid functions
to perform given the capital formation and job-
creating goals that we set for ourselves. However,
we had to make one choice of a course of action from
a wide menu of choices and, for various reasons, this
was the choice that we made at this specific time.

Like all strategic decisions, it was a value-
laden judgment based on our perception of what we
felt that we could accomplish given the temper of the
times, the funding available to us, and potential
political and administrative linkages and conflicts.
Moreover, the decision was not a mutually exclusive
decision; we could pursue this alternative plus a
series of other courses of action based first on the
desires of the affected target population and second
on other external realities. The possibility of success was one of these key realities. Better to succeed in a small way than not to succeed at all.

Thus, although we recognized that our definition
of the problem and our response to it was far narrower than its reality, we stuck with this definition
for a great number of reasons:

(1) Although unemployment in the ghetto ex-
    tends to all age groups, we believed that
    a program dealing with the 17-26 age group
    would have the greatest chance of success.
    This group, because of its relative youth,
    is somewhat less alienated and discouraged

than the older, long-term unemployed. Because of this, they might respond more
quickly to the opportunity for employment
even at the entry-level. The over-26
group, because of past discouragement and
open prejudice, were, we believed, less
apt to believe the promises of anything
other than menial-type jobs and thus might
create a difficult staffing problem for
the newly expanded industrial plants.

(2) The females in the 17-26 age group are,
in all probability, homebound mothers of
small children. Although creating jobs
for them is most desirable, child day-care
centers and other facilities or arrangements are essential to the success of a
program aimed at this particular target
group. We did not then want to get involved in a whole series of expensive and
hard-to-mount support programs. These
support programs would have to be provided
at a later date, preferably by the city's
Department of Social Services.

(3) As discussed earlier in this chapter, we
hypothesized the need for the creation of
long-term entry-level jobs to take care
of successive waves of 17-26-year-old
males. Because of this, we wanted to con-
centrate our initial efforts on programs
geared to the needs of these young.

The locus of the problem, as we perceived it, was
at the city level. Prior efforts had been mounted to
determine the true cause of the out-migration from the
city of a significant number of industrial firms. However, no one at the city level had proposed the creation of a city-wide economic development effort aimed
at curbing this out-migration. Based upon a series
of macro-economic studies that dealt intelligently
with a range of economic factors, the undesirability
of the city as an industrial site was presumed. The
error in these past studies, in our opinion, was an
avoidance of a direct confrontation with the managerial

decision-making process. As will be discussed later,
our research into the causes of the problem relied
heavily upon perceived managerial behavior as opposed to a more rigid economic analysis.

Last, we recognized that the problem of unemployment had both substantive and procedural overtones.
As the focus of the solution to the problem of the
lack of entry-level industrial jobs, the creation of
new industrial sites would require the intensive cooperation of those city agencies whose prior behavior
had influenced the out-migration of the industrial
firm. Zoning regulations, code enforcement procedures
and construction ordinances, to cite but a few examples, are some of the procedural problems with which
an economic development must deal. Many of these ordinances and administrative rulings are archaic. Others
are irrelevant to the task of economic development.
We recognized that part of our task would be to convince the members of other city agencies of the wisdom of amending or abolishing those regulations
provided that they were not in conflict with values
superior to the need for a reindustrialization of
specific portions of the city. By doing so, we also
hoped to stimulate a wholesale review of the legal
constraints placed on many social and economic activities within the city. Ideally, we were looking
for a way to redefine the concept of a city government, and the responsibility to the individual of
this government.

THE CAUSES OF THE PROBLEM

Core-city under-employment and unemployment can
be related to any number of factors depending solely
on the rationale underlying the analysis. Within the
context of this discussion, however, we can consider
the flight from the core city of both large and small
industrial firms as the basic cause of the present
lack of city-based entry-level industrial jobs. The
reason for choosing this factor in explanation of the
cause-effect relations to be explored is its cogency
to the proposed projects: industrial parks. Other
causes of the lack of entry-level jobs can be

described, but these descriptions are not, in all
likelihood, directly relevant to an analysis of the
need for an industrial development project. That
they might be relevant to another problem is significant, in a logical way, only to that problem!

The basic cause of the problem which is the focus
of our project, however, has a number of underlying
causes. Indeed, the flight from the city of the industrial firm is the outcome of a series of very fundamental interactions amongst the socio-economic
characteristics of the city. The task of this phase
of the planning process is to pick out only those
causes or interactions that are most relevant to a
justification of the need for the proposed industrial
park, and the support programs needed to guarantee
the success of the industrial park. For example:

(1) The age and condition of most core-city
industrial plants is a factor that has helped to
stimulate the exodus of industrial plants from the
core city to the suburbs. Most of these plants are
from 30-70 years of age, old multi-story buildings
that are physically inconsistent with present modes
of production. In many instances, it is cheaper to
relocate than to renovate an old, decrepit building.

(2) Although many of those firms that moved
out of the city would have preferred to remain close
to their original location because of the external
economies provided by the city, the lack of suitable
land for modern plant construction, the cost of that
land when available, and the costs of core-city construction further served to force their hands. Substantive evidence in support of this contention can
be gained empirically.

(3) The inability of the highly skilled worker
who is more apt to live in the suburbs to commute
into the core-city plant has further aggravated the
plant-location decision. Public transportation from
the suburbs to the core city is either lacking or
inadequate. Commuting to the core city by car is
equally troublesome. Although a suburban location
is untenable for the unskilled laborer because of

short-cycle or non-existent learning curves for unskilled labor, management is not normally concerned
with his preferences. The more critical factor is
the preferences of the skilled labor and managerial
group.

(4) The quality and the motivation of the core
city unskilled laborer is less than that of the unskilled suburban or rural laborer. Part of this is
due to the environmental factors which surround the
ghetto-bound laborer, such as a poor, almost irrelevant education system which in many core cities now
produces generations of "functional illiterates."
Although the skills requirements for many entry-leve
jobs are low, certain social requirements must still
be met by the prospective employee: the ability to
properly complete job applications, pass some form
of qualifying test, adjust to the discipline of work
and so forth. Given normal levels of unemployment,
the typical employer will try to avoid this type of
personnel problem by moving to a suburban, or even
rural location. The deterioration of most core-city
educational systems is a factor which is just now
receiving recognition from the businessman. The los
of this external economy, and the effect on the potential labor force of this loss, is a most critical
factor.

To all of these causes, others can be added:
overt, covert, recognized and unrecognized racial
discrimination; archaic zoning and code enforcement
regulations; the lack of vital external economies
such as adequate police and fire protection; an un-
stable political climate resulting in capricious
and arbitrary tax rates, etc. In general, all of
these causes relate to the problems of economic development because of the scope of concerns involved
in this type of activity. This broad a cause-effect
relationship may not, however, obtain the rationale needed to justify another type of project or
program, such as the need for supplementary educatic
programs, recreational areas, developments, and so
forth. In each instance, however, the causes identified as basic to the problem should be directly
relevant both to the problem that is to be solved,

and the program or project that is proposed as the
solution to the problem. Narrowing down statements
of cause-effect relationships, however, is difficult
because of the many perspectives from which the problem can be viewed. Nonetheless, a narrow perspective
is essential for program planning since the foremost
task of program planning is the creation of a project
that will make a significant contribution to the solution of a problem. A complete understanding of all
of the causes of the problem is not essential in this
pragmatic process.

THE DATA NEEDED TO PLAN

The data needed to plan are basically a function
of the nature of the problem to be solved and the
"state of the art" of the concern of society for the
problem under study. The amount and the technical
validity of the data that must be collected similarly
is a function of the problem to be solved. The data
collection process is also constrained by the need
for either perfect or imperfect knowledge of the problem, and all of the factors that created the problem.

In the instance of our proposed industrial development, only a few pieces of information were essential in explication of the problem:

(1) The lack of entry-level jobs in the city,
as evidenced by 250,000 unemployed persons, most of whom are black or Spanish-
speaking Americans; and

(2) The gradual decrease in the size and the
vitality of the industrial base of the city.

Both of these points had been documented in earlier studies of the City of New York. We in Model
Cities merely had to accept the validity of this information and its relevance to our interests to decide on the need for an economic development program.

As one digs deeper into the causes of a problem,
however, the data that must be collected become more

specific, particularly if these data are to be used
in finding a specific solution to a specific problem
For example:

(1) An overwhelming portion of the industrial
base of the City of New York is made up of relativel
small firms employing between 40-60 persons. These
firms are apparently tied to the city because of the
external economies that an urban location offers to
such firms. The first bit of information here was
once again available from city sources. The second
bit of information was dependent upon an understanding of the economics of the plan location problems.

(2) In most instances, the most critical external economy that an urban location offers--and th
is especially true in New York--is an abundance of
low-cost, low-skill labor. Many of the firms remain
ing in the city do so despite cramped, substandard
facilities, poor transportation networks, and inadequate public services. To them, the quick availabil
ity of inexpensive labor is the critical factor in
their location decision.

This information was not found in any availabl
studies. Rather, it was determined empirically by
interviewing the executives of a number of firms in
order to determine their reasons for remaining in Ne
York City. Although many answers were given to this
question, the predominant answer was the availabilit
of a low-cost labor force. The substantial availabi
ity of a large pool of personnel as compensation for
high turnover rates was also cited as a key reason
for remaining in the city. Although this raises a
number of moral issues having to do with the possibl
exploitation of an unskilled labor force, these issu
are not relevant to the present analysis.

(3) Even more critical to understanding the pr
posed project is the fact that many of these firms
feel that their growth potential is severely limited
by the availability of adequate manufacturing facilities. Were proper quarters made available to them,
they would be able to expand the size of their operations to meet observed market demand and, in doing

so, create additional jobs for the unskilled and the
semi-skilled laborer. Once again, this information
was picked up in a series of interviews with corporate executives. The validity of the information was,
in each case, verified by an analysis of the respondent
firm's balance sheet and profit-and-loss statement.
In other words, specific evidence of profitable growth
as evidenced by the past history of the firm was sought
after. Many of the firms have this growth potential.
For their size, they are over-capitalized and thus this
over-capitalization is the result of the firm's inability to profitably reinvest past earnings in its own operation and the lack of willingness of these firms to
invest their capital in outside businesses.

(4) In addition, these firms are aware of the
problem involved in hiring urban minority-group members. These groups have been the backbone of much of
the core-city labor force for some time now and the
employers--particularly those in the 40-60 man plant--
know how to adapt to the characteristics of this group,
provide appropriate training to them, and deal with the
manifest problems of the poor. This is not to suggest
that these employers desire to deal with this type of
problem, but rather that they are willing to do so if
this willingness will help them protect their own business interests. Once again, this data was gained in
field trips. Plants were inspected in order to determine the percentage of the labor force that was drawn
from the black American and Spanish-speaking American
population. We needed to know whether or not a prospective employer would, indeed, hire a Negro and
whether or not he would provide a decent job for this
employee. Inspection trips through various plants were
made, and data on wage scales were collected and an-
analyzed.

In our opinion, the data that we have outlined
are sufficient for general planning purposes. First,
the data are relevant to the problem of unemployment.
Second, there is an abundance of reinforcing data
available from other sources because of the state of
the art of the concern for the unemployed. They have
been studied and restudied, indeed over-studied. This
concern, of course, may not be found in the instance

of other sub-sets of problems, i.e., the need for co
tinuing education programs, new recreational areas
in the ghetto, small-scale transportation systems,
and so forth. In cases where the problem is not wel
understood, or where there has been no real public
concern for the problem, the data collection and
analysis process can be tedious, frustrating, and of
ten useless. To some extent, in fact, the narrower
the problem to be attacked, and the narrower the solution to the problem that is to be invoked, the les
available may be the required data.

This does not negate the need for a data collection and analysis process. First, the existence and
the relevance of the problem should be proved where
it is humanly possible to do so. Second, once the
reality of the problem has been established, the pos
sibility of solving the problem also should be carefully and thoroughly documented. Last, the problem
and its solution should be congruent. Short-term
solutions to long-term problems are, in general, invalid except where political visibility is essential

In a similar vein, we did not feel that the nature of the general problem that we were attempting
to attack required the collection of massive or detailed sums of information. The problem of unemploy
ment is all to visible; much is already known of its
causes and effects. We were looking for an entry
point into an immediate solution to a narrowly defin
problem as opposed to a global solution to a broadly
defined problem. Our scope and our aspirations were
limited. The rationale for this limited view of our
proposed project was quite simple; the funds available for Model Cities implementation are so limited
as to presently suggest only a series of demonstration projects. If we could provide the data that
proved the need, and later the viability of but one
industrial park, we would then have generated a proj
ect capable of utilizing a major portion of the fund
available to the Model Cities program for economic
development. Although, in theory, the total need fo
industrial development in the city should be documented, and a master plan for this economic development worked out, the practicality of the present

situation calls for a simpler approach. Prove the
feasibility of but one project, preferably with
private-sector financial support, and then try to
stimulate private-sector initiative to follow the
initial lead! As they begin to follow the lead, work
out a master plan that optimizes the effect of this
private-sector behavior.*

In addition to the general data that we collected
by the rather simple expedient of knocking on doors,
we also sought the answers to the following questions:

(1) Is there sufficient land available in
New York for the development of a series
of industrial parks?

(2) If there is, is it possible to purchase
this land at a price low enough to make
the total developmental package financially feasible?

(3) What are the economic, social, and political impediments to these actions?

We answered the first question by checking City
Planning Commission maps, by reviewing prior economic
studies of New York City, and by personally visiting
areas that looked promising. We found that there was
indeed suitable land available, although the sizes of

---

*As might be expected, this section of the chap-
ter created an author's controversy. The statement
on the "abandoning of low-cost, low-skill labor" is
the center of the concern since this statement can
be correctly viewed only from the perspective of the
employer. From the point of view of the work force,
these low wage scales can be regarded as unjustifi-
ably subsidizing the cost structure of otherwise inefficient firms--something that the minority groups
would understandably regard as reprehensible. We
must agree with them if this is indeed true, but the
evidence in support or refutation of this point is
beyond the scope of this book.

the potential sites were as small as one acre and as
large as 100 acres. In addition, we gained first-hand
knowledge of the effects on parts of New York City of
generations of uncontrolled economic and real estate
development, and the blight that this development had
created in the Brooklyn and Bronx boroughs of New
York. Much valuable land in New York is now occupied
by junk yards, old garages, lofts, and similar low-
output forms of land usage. Residential dwellings in
poor conditions are scattered throughout many of these
industrial areas, worn-down and ill-used despite the
inherent value of the land on which they sit. The
economic possibilities for the rehabilitation of many
of these poorly used areas are fantastic, but little
is being done now to realize this vast potential. As
our research showed, the inner city offers the smalle
firm a number of critical external economies such as
a large supply of relatively inexpensive labor. Until
such time as local government has the will power to
deal with this rehabilitative process on a reasonably
large scale, however, this great opportunity for a
central city industrial renaissance will be lost.

As we dug deeper into the problem it also became
increasingly evident that large-scale industrial park
were beyond the fiscal and planning capabilities of
the city, particularly if the major funds to be used
for this task were to come from future Model Cities
appropriations. Conversely, we found that a large
number of 1-3-acre sites were available within the
target area. Because of their size, these sites can
be used most effectively for the type of small-scale
industrial plant that is found in abundance in most
core cities. The stated market value of this land,
however, is beyond the price that most small firms
can afford. Although much of this land now remains
unused, the landowners fully recognize the real and
potential squeeze on land that is now being created
within the city and are unwilling to sell except at
an extremely advantageous price. Because of this,
we realized that small industrial developments of the
type that we had begun to visualize would be impossible except where the land could be made available
to the new purchaser at a more favorable price. Land
value write-down procedures were suggested. Although
this technique has been used in other cities, we were

told that the New York City government objected to
this technique if the purpose behind the purchase was
the conveyance of the land to an industrial firm.

Despite this, we soon found that the city could
purchase the land and, by turning it over to a city-
controlled and non-profit corporation, construct a
building on this land that could be leased to an industrial firm. In this instance, the cost of the
lease would include as payment in lieu of taxes a 7
per cent interest factor on the written-down value
of the land. The building as non-city property would
then be taxed on the normal basis, with the tenant
required to pay this real estate tax. Upon expiration
of the lease, the rights to the property would revert
first to the non-profit corporation and then to the
city, with this last conveyance being the consideration granted to the city for its prior write-down of
the value of the land.

Despite all of this, land write-down procedures
are virtually impossible to accomplish. In the case
of New York, the approval of the City Planning Commission, the city's Economic Development Administration, the City Bureau of the Budget and a special
Mayor's Committee are essential. In addition, if the
land in question is not presently zoned for industrial
use, rezoning procedures must also be undertaken. Because of the possibility of public intervention this
last task can be nigh unto impossible.

Land write-down procedures, however, make 1-3-acre
industrial developments most attractive. Because of
this, we in Model Cities joined hands with the other
city agencies that had expressed an interest in this
type of project. As a result of this joint effort, we
found that we could finance the construction of a
30,000 to 60,000-square-foot building and make it
available at $1.15 to $1.20 per foot rental on a 20-
year lease. This was possible in 1967-68, despite
rates of interest of from 6 per cent to 8 per cent
on most of the financing segments.

Last, the proposed small-site developments project also avoided a problem which had been brought to
our attention by community leaders: the opposition in

1967 to large-scale ghetto-based industrial parks by
ghetto residents. Previous attempts to develop such
a concept in New York City had failed because of citizen opposition. We were told that any new attempt
would be similarly opposed.* The small-scale development, because it could be accomplished in predominant
ly industrialized areas or on substantial land near
a residential area, could probably avoid overt citizen complaint. The last bit of information served
to reinforce the notion of small-scale development
programs, although we had originally thought only in
terms of large-scale developments.

STATEMENT OF GOALS AND APPROACHES

The creation of entry-level industrial jobs thus
was the task that we had set for ourselves. The target group for this program was to be the 17-26-year-
old male resident of the Model Cities area. The
function that we proposed to perform in attainment o𝚏
this goal was the development of a series of small-
scale industrial developments into which suitable
smaller industrial firms would relocate. We were als
prepared to offer, as an inducement to the interested
industrial firm, city-sponsored manpower training and
development programs.

Our goals were, in part, predetermined. We were
aware of a critical and admittedly obvious need: jobs
We were also aware of a need to make the core city a
more desirable site location for the small-scale industrial firm that forms the backbone of most urbanized industrial areas. For this project, data
collection was not a problem; information on needs
was available. Our primary need was for an assessmer
of the true interest that the smaller manufacturer
would show in support of such a project, and whether

---

*We understand that large-scale industrial sites
would now (1969) be acceptable. To our mind this is
evidence of the growing awareness of the ghetto-boun𝚍
on the possibilities for social and economic growth
that are now becoming available to them.

or not an adequate financing package could be developed. It was for this reason that most of our data collection procedures were empirically oriented. Although our statement of goals was concise, we recognized that our project would do more than simply create entry-level jobs. If we were successful, unemployment rates would decrease, real income in the city would increase, and the city would be made a more viable place in which to live. This spot-renewal technique could also be expected to stimulate private-sector interest in ghetto-based, profit-oriented rehabilitation enterprises. In other words, Model Cities would provide the seed money that would help to attract broader private-sector interest in the ghetto. One of the unstated goals of our project was to prove that the city was still industrially viable and not, as alleged by others, subject to a slow, but nonetheless certain, death.

Much of our statement of goals was, and is, value-oriented. Our entire concept of an anti-poverty program was colored by our conviction that an anti-poverty program is, in its broadest context, a large-scale socialization process. Ply the culturally and economically deprived with a series of products and services that help them to feel more self-confident of their ability to successfully structure their lives. Provide them with jobs and incomes so that they can develop their own internalized demands for essential social welfare services. Provide them with the income so that they can purchase these essential services from the private sector. The poor want the opportunity to behave and act like anybody else. They want to buy or receive essential social services on the same basis as do the middle class. The reason for focusing on capital formation was our way of saying that this is an essential first step in the socialization process. Because we spoke openly about the socialization process, we recognized that much of our interpretation of data would be value-oriented.

Clearly, there are alternative ways in which entry-level jobs can be created within a highly developed urban economy. Most of these techniques, however, are beyond the scope of action normally available

to a city. For example, a city can offer to subsi-
dize the costs of training personnel for entry-level
industrial jobs by absorbing some or all of the
learning-curve costs for a firm wishing to expand its
labor force. Or a city government can finance the
cost of new equipment at lower than market rates of
interest provided that this equipment is used for
expansion purposes. Tax advantages may also be given
to those industrial firms that embark on an expansion
program. Any combination of these three approaches,
plus others that we have not specified, can be used
to stimulate in-city industrial growth. Most of these
techniques did not become available until recently.

We avoided these alternative approaches because
of our concern with their legal feasibility. Each of
these actions implies the granting by the city of
preferential treatment to a specific firm. The rationale for this preferential treatment is not politically obvious especially since the industrial firm
does not appear to be providing some consideration to
the city for this preferred position. In the case of
the new industrial site, however, the sponsored indus
trial firm will have to absorb the increased overhead
of its expanded quarters. In general, the increase
will be both relative and absolute: relative in that
the rental cost per square foot of plant will increas
absolute in that the total rent will increase both be
cause of the increase in the size of the plant and
the increase in the rental rate. Last, the firm must
agree to a 20-25-year lease that effectively creates
a marriage between the industrial firm and the city.
No other technique that we know of can wed the industrial firm to the city for so extended a period of
time. Our sub-goal of at least three to five generations of entry-level jobs is secured by the length of
the lease which the industrial firm must accept as
their part of the bargain.

TYPE OF PROJECTS OR ACTIONS DESIRED

We could not find evidence suggesting that any
economic development project of this type had ever
before seen proposed or attempted. This, however,

was not the key motivation for our proposal. Rather,
we felt that this type of project was vitally needed
because of:

(1) The private and public sector linkages
    that the program would provide;
(2) The experience that it would provide to
    those city personnel whose active in-
    volvement would be needed for a successful multi-agency cooperative effort;
(3) The evidence of this inter-agency effort;
(4) The political visibility of the program;
(5) The fact that the program, once general
    financing operating procedures had been
    established, could be routinized and
    replicated in other areas of the city;
(6) The fact that only a few members of the
    Model Cities would be required to main-
    tain the program; and
(7) The fact that the program could be expected
    to show repeated successes.

In addition, we were convinced that the program would
provide other significant economic benefits to the
city. One proposal, for example, called for the purchase of a 60,000-square-foot site for $142,000 and its
subsequent write-down to $42,000. A $300,000 building
would then be put onto this site. For an initial out-
of-pocket investment of $100,000, a minimum of 30 new
jobs would be created, and the wage scales of the
original 60 people employed by the firm would be upgraded. On expiration of the lease, the city would
receive title to the property. Last, its present tax
interest in the property would be increased by the
assessed value of the new building.

All of these factors taken together suggest a minimum return of 40 per cent per year on the city's investment of $100,000: $15,000 in new real estate
taxes; the preservation of about $10,000 in existing
city payroll taxes (this assumes that the firm would
move out of the city if new space were not provided
for it); plus a reduction in income maintenance subsidies to the unemployed of at least $60,000-$90,000
per year. Regardless of the analytic technique

employed, the present value of the prospective financial return to the city was substantial.

The benefit to the leasing firm was equally substantial: a new plant built to its specifications
and at a price that it can afford; access to a large
pool of labor; the economies in production costs that
a new plant provides; and the present worth of the
projected expansion in sales volume and profit.
Everyone appears to profit from a project of this
type: the city, the employer, and the employee, both
present and prospective.

The time needed to complete the project was one
year: an initial planning phase plus the time needed
for site preparation and construction. The project
itself is not dependent upon any other project and
can proceed at its own pace without slowing down the
progress of any other Model Cities project.

FACTORS THAT EXPEDITE OR RETARD
PROJECT EXECUTION

Two critical factors can be expected to retard a
project of this type:

(1) The need to gain the complete cooperation and
    approval of those city agencies whose approv
    al is needed for a project of this type; and

(2) The need to arrange private sector financing
    for the proposed building.

In addition, skilled management consulting advice
is needed to evaluate the present and projected finan
cial strength of the lessee. Since the purpose of th
program is to provide jobs, and the availability of
these jobs is dependent upon management's ability to
manage, the Model Cities staff will need continued
access to people capable of evaluating the business
prospects of any prospective lessee. An error in
judgment on the future business prospects of the les
see can leave the lessee with a larger plant to support but with no increase in sales income or profit

support this increased expenditure. Because of this
extra burden, the city can be left with a financially
weakened tenant. If this happens, the Model Cities
residents will still be left without the jobs they
were promised. This possibility needs to be minimized.

Conversely, the legal and financing problems presented by a project such as this have to be solved
only once. Once the first project is completed, the
Model Cities staff need only follow the procedures
that have already been established and repeat the
project as desired. Admittedly, each project will
have to be tailored to fit the specific needs both
of the client and the workers, but in general the
overall process can pretty well be routinized.

Additional problems will be encountered in the
recruitment of the expanded labor force by the new
tenant. This task can be undertaken by the city's
manpower training group, elements of the anti-poverty
effort, or the neighborhood service centers. For
the recruiting to be successful, of course, the industrial firm must be able to offer the prospective
employees satisfactory working conditions and realistic wage scales. These two factors must also be
evaluated carefully by the management consultants
retained to advise the Model Cities group. One of
the requirements that the prospective tenant must be
able to reasonably guarantee is his ability to pay
satisfactory wages. The management consultant must
be as certain of this factor as is possible. Further,
the consultant must be able to evaluate the industrial firm's behavior toward minority groups in order
to avoid accepting promises of future action that are
essentially meaningless. Carefully conducted plant
visits will provide first-hand evidence of past behavior and attitudes, but these attitudes should be
probed deeply and thoroughly in a series of discussions.

COST-BENEFIT ANALYSIS

As noted earlier, the primary out-of-pocket cost
incurred in a project of this type is the difference

between the market price of the land and the written-down value later placed on it and recovered over the term of the lease. Based upon 1-3-acre sites, this net out-of-pocket cost will vary between $50,000 to $100,000 dependent solely on the amount of the write-down needed to bring the total cost of the land and building into line with a long-term leasehold cost that the manufacturing firm can legitimately afford. Staff and consulting costs will also be incurred in the development of the total project. The staff cost will vary based on the number of projects undertaken, although an estimate of 200 hours of Model Cities staff time per project is not unreasonable. An additional 200 hours of time will have to be logged on the project by the representatives of those other city agencies that must cooperate in the actual imple mentation of the project. Thus, based on an average annual wage scale of $18,000, staff cost per project can be expected to be $4,000 to $5,000. Consultant time per project is a likely input with the variance dependent upon the complexity of the business organi-zation that must be evaluated. Depending upon the caliber of consulting help needed, a cost of between $1,000 to $4,000 per project should be anticipated. The client's costs, of course, are not relevant to this analysis since he is expected to absorb them as his contribution to the undertaking.

Based upon a sampling of economic development projects, the annual rate of return that can be expected from projects of this type will vary from a low 50 per cent to 60 per cent to a high of between 300 per cent and 400 per cent. This is the calcul-able monetary value of the project. Certain non-monetary benefits will also be provided by the project The factors producing these benefits, some of which have already been mentioned, are the following:

(1) The increased property taxes accruing to the city as a result of the construc-tion of a new building on heretofore unused land;

(2) The increase in payroll taxes (in the spe-cific case of New York) resulting from the number of new jobs created, and the

increase in salaries to those presently
employed personnel whose work skills
will be upgraded as a result of a corporate expansion;

(3) The multiplied effect upon the city's economy of these increased wage scales;

(4) The decrease in the city's share of the
income maintenance payments made to the
unemployed;

(5) The decrease in the costs of the related
social services that will no longer be
required by the previously unemployed;
and

(6) The present value of the market value of the
land and buildings when their ownership
reverts to the city upon termination of
the lease.

Many of these benefits can, of course, be monetized with only a moderate degree of accuracy. We
would maintain, however, that complete accuracy in
predicting benefits is not necessary and may even be
misleading on an investment of this type because of
the high value of the projected rates of return. However, this statement applies only to projects of this
type wherein the annual monetized return on investment
exceeds 50 per cent to 60 per cent. This statement
should not be applied to projects of dissimilar content and particularly community maintenance programs
from which no measurable short-term financial benefit
can be anticipated.

In any cost-benefit analysis, specific project
costs and specific project benefits will have to be
routinely calculated. We believe that it is wiser
to err on the low side when predicting benefits and
on the high side when anticipating costs. This rule
is particularly relevant to those projects or programs
which are categorized as overhead costs. Overhead
programs, however, should never be sacrificed simply
because they provide no immediately perceivable financial benefit. In our opinion, they are necessary to
legitimize a heavy portion of those programs that do
have financially calculable outputs. Without them,
those programs with projected financial returns may

not receive the ready acceptance from the target
group that is essential to their success.

If a support program is essential to the success
of a basic program, its costs and benefits should be
calculated along with the costs and benefits attrib-
utable to the basic program. For example, if an industrial firm will move into the city only if a
manpower training program is tied in with an industrial site program, the costs of this training program must then be added to the site development costs
in order to arrive at the full costs of the program.
From a realistic point of view, the training costs
may be regarded as an overhead cost that support the
site development projects. However, the benefits
provided by each component of the program can be calculated separately if so desired, although this seems
a needless and irrelevant complication.

A cost and benefit analysis should ideally be
calculated for every program or project that is undertaken. Simply because a project or program is placed
into an overhead category, or because the benefits
provided by a project cannot be stated in monetary
terms, does not mean that benefits cannot or should
not be calculated for the project.

For example, a block workers' project whose focus
is on encouraging target group citizens to participate
in Model Cities sponsored programs provides a vast ar-
ray of social benefits, none of which can be described
in monetary terms. By getting the target area citizen
to take a more active role in the society around him,
this type of program may provide the following types
of benefits:

> (1) Improved health for the area resi-
>   dents--by getting them to utilize
>   available health services in the
>   community;
> (2) Improved housing--by convincing them
>   of the need for cooperative efforts
>   in dealing with stubborn landlords;

     (3) Increased political power--by simply get-
         ting out the vote as evidence of their
         concern with the political environment
         in which they live; and
     (4) A decrease in juvenile delinquency--by
         getting them to attend PTA and other
         school meetings as evidence of a greater
         concern with the educational well-being
         of their children.

Although these benefits cannot be stated in financial terms, they can still be measured in both the
short term and the long term. The statement of benefits even in the non-monetary terms provides a way of
measuring the output of the program. Because these
outputs are basically concerned with the socialization process, the benefits provided by most overhead
programs should be stated in terms of measures of the
socialization process.

Quite obviously, the choice between programs with
a financial output and those without a financial output is a high-level policy decision. This policy
should reflect an awareness of the characteristics of
the community, and its need for those programs which
seek to counteract the culture of poverty. Jobs alone
will not do the trick. A person needs to be healthy
enough to work; he needs help in solving many basic
family problems before he can become an adequate
worker; and he needs an adequate education. Projects
designed to accomplish these ends should not be sacrificed simply because they do not provide benefits
expressible in economic terms.

THE FUNDING OF A PROGRAM

Except in those rare instances where the client
is a large, well-known national firm, funding site
development projects can be tediously complex. In
the case of a large firm, its credit rating is normally sufficient security for the substantial long-
term loan that will be needed to purchase the site and
construct the required building. In the case of a

smaller firm, however, this type of security is lacking. Because of this, the lending institution must
look for some other form of security as the basis for
its loan.

In general, lending institutions will assert
their need for a properly secured position by limiting the size of their loan to a relatively small proportion of the value of the total project. For
example, we proposed in one New York project to purchase 60,000 square feet of land for $142,000 and
then write its value down to $42,000. The building
to be constructed on half of the 60,000-square-foot
lot was estimated reliably to cost $300,000. One in-
terested bank offered to provide a 40 per cent <u>first</u>
mortgage, or $140,000, on the new value of $342,000
created by this total land and building package.

Thus, of a total out-of-pocket cost of $442,000:

    (1) $142,000 would be provided by the City of
         New York, or a designated agency of the
         city for the purchase of the land;
    (2) $140,000 would be provided by a private-
         sector lending institution, in this case
         a commercial bank;
    (3) Other sources would be required to provide
         the remaining $160,000. In developing
         this project, we were able to get a
         $40,000 commitment from the prospective
         lessee, plus $120,000 in commitments
         from New York State economic development
         agencies and the federal Small Business
         Administration (SBA). These last three
         commitments completed the package.

However, the bank insisted on a first lien, i.e.,
its interests were to be satisfied first in the event
of a default. The SBA was then willing to take a
second position behind the bank. The city, however,
was required to take a fourth, or last position, a
rather difficult one for it to justify because of the
size of its investment in the project and because the
lease payments on the property were based on the
written-down value of the land and not its original

value. In other words, the city cannot recover its
$100,000 write-down investment during the term of the
lease. It may only recoup this sum after the termination date of the original lease and any renewals,
and then only if residual value of the total package
of land and buildings is in excess of $100,000. Thus,
the city is the key risk-taker in a project of this
type. Although the new tenant assumes an increased
business risk in contracting for the larger, more
expensive facility, he does so because he is convinced of the effect of this move upon his sales and
profit picture. If nothing else, this type of project underscores the critical nature of the risks and
uncertainties that are inherent in an economic development project. The pay-off on a successful economic
development project is sufficiently high, however,
to justify the time and the effort which must be
placed into it.

Different types of Model Cities projects will,
of course, require different funding mixes. Some
projects may be entirely reliant upon funds put together by the Community Development Agency. The individual funding sources to whom the CDA will turn
can be expected to establish their own timetables for
the grant review and acceptance process. Similarly,
each of the funding sources will place various constraints on the project before they grant it final
approval. In the example that we have cited, the bank
limited its involvement in the project to $140,000,
although its commitment was for a period of twenty
years.

In this example, permanent capital funds are
needed on a non-recurring basis. The Model Cities
program, or a relevant city agency, must provide the
seed money which, in specific cases, may be demonstration funds. Conversely, in a project such as this,
there are no reimbursable or revolving funds. Each
project is, in essence, a "one-shot" deal.

STRATEGY FOR ACHIEVING GOALS

The fundamental strategy that was developed and
pursued in the projected economic development programs

that we are discussing was presented earlier in this
chapter. For very obvious reasons, we had to adopt
a collaborative strategy:

(1) The success of projects of this type is
heavily dependent upon a strong private sector-public
sector relationship. First, prospective industrial
tenants must be found who can meet a series of critical economic and socio-economic criteria. Second,
a viable city-tenant relationship must then be established with these prospective tenants. Last, private
sector funds must then be made available to complete
the financing of the project.

(2) During the time that the public-private
sector relationship is being established, similar
working arrangements must be developed between a
number of interested and involved city agencies. Potential conflicts between these agencies must be resolved.

(3) Last, because of the financing mix, city-
state and city-federal relationships must also be
developed. This is especially necessary when each
of the different levels of government have to reach
an accord on the scope of their participation in each
individual project, and their respective financial
positions vis-à-vis each other and the private-sector
lending institutions.

Clearly, there is no room for unresolved conflicts
in a project such as this. Firm commitments are needed, commitments that will not be revoked once they are
made.

Equally essential to project success is the approval of the residents of the target area. First,
the federal laws creating the anti-poverty and Model
Cities programs call for the involvement of the poor
in the planning and administrative process. They
should be part of the decision-making process that
passes on any Model Cities project. If they fail to
see the value of a project and refuse to ratify the
request for funds, the project should be dropped, although not without an attempt to educate the target

area residents on both the risks and the benefits
provided by the project.

Second, the success of an economic development
project rests heavily upon the availability of a motivated labor force. The target area group should
have the right of first refusal on these jobs. To
make this right a real one, the neighborhood service
centers in the target area should be aware of the opportunity well in advance of others and be fully prepared to recruit and screen the type of labor force
needed by the new industrial facility. Indeed, the
neighborhood service center should accept this responsibility as part of their contribution to the
program. This will help to legitimize the project
to those target area residents who are not personally involved in either the planning or the administration of the community renewal effort. Last, the
neighborhood service center should accept the responsibility in order to build bridges with the industrial
community in their area for the long-term benefits
that such a relationship can provide. Many firms have
left urbanized areas because of the inadequacy or lack
of manufacturing facilities. Others have left because
they were unable, or believed that they were unable,
to recruit and hold onto an economically viable labor
force. Others have left because they had no relationship with the community and, therefore, no reason for
staying. Finally, other industrial firms have left
urban locations because of the mistrust that has built
up over the years between them and their minority-
group neighbors with whom they had little or no dia-
logue.

As our research suggests, many of these firms
would have gladly remained in the city if an effort
had been made by the administration to make them feel
welcome and, indeed, desired. The external economics
provided by an urban area such as the ready availability of a labor force are persuasive realities for any
industrial firm. But they are not the type of realities that the executives of a small or moderately
sized firm have time to explore. They tend to take
the availability of a labor force for granted. These
busy executives oftentimes need to be reminded of the

community's relationship to their firm, the mutual
support that each one can provide the other, and the
real benefits of this support. This "reminding"
should be the task of properly selected and properly
trained target area groups supervised, initially at
least, by Model Cities staff personnel.

Thus, a project of this type will require the
collaboration of a great many groups and a great many
people. It will also require a vast amount of technical skills which will need to be supplemented by
people-oriented skills. The broader the base of involvement in the project, the more acceptable and successful it is apt to be. Political ties and friend-
ships are as essential to its success as are business
or economic skills.

TIMETABLE

Based on our New York experience, and presuming
no legal or administrative impediments to a project
such as this, six months' time should be allowed for
an economic development team to generate its first
project. Not only must the cooperation of a full
range of city agencies and community action groups
be gained, but--and this is more time-consuming--
appropriate tenants must be found for whom appropriate sites can be selected. If a detailed building
design phase is needed, an additional three months
may be used up before construction begins.

Once the first project has been worked out, however, additional projects can be brought in just as
quickly as staff capabilities will allow. The delay-
ing factor here will be the length of time that is
needed to locate suitable and willing tenants. It is
good tenants, not funding, that can be expected to
be in short supply.

MEASURING ANTICIPATED RESULTS

The results anticipated from a program should, of
course, be directly related to the goals set for the

program. In the case of our proposed economic development project, the results of the project must
first be measured in terms of the new capital brought
into the area, and then the number of entry-level
jobs created by each project. If a cost effectiveness measure is desired, the cost per entry-level job
created by the industrial site process can be meaningfully compared to the cost of creating a similar
number of jobs using other devices such as manpower
training programs. A cross-sectional cost-
effectiveness measure can be obtained by comparing
the costs and benefits provided by a series of industrial site development projects.

If the goals of a project are stated in simple terms, the technique for measuring the results
may be equally simple: periodic counts of the increases in the labor force using the size of the pre-
project labor force as the relevant base. If, however,
the stated goals of the project are more complex,
measures for each sub-set of the statement of goals
must be determined. For example, one of the projected goals for an industrial development project may be
its supposed effect on real estate values in the surrounding area. In this case, real estate values for
the area should be established prior to the project,
and checked periodically afterwards for any change
that might be related to the existence of the project.
Because an increase in real estate values is related
to a multiplicity of factors, however, a simple cause-
effect relationship can neither be defined nor proven.
At best, descriptive statements on the qualitative
increase in neighboring real estate values may be
made.

A simple statement of goals does not necessarily
mean that the measures of anticipated results are easily obtained or, even if obtained, meaningful. For
example, one of the results anticipated for a block
workers' program could very well be an increase in
the utilization of already available medical care facilities. Conceivably, this greater use could be
measured by accepting the hospital's out-patient visit
figures provided that there had been no change in the
period under question in other health-related factors,

such as a flu epidemic that might have temporarily
swelled demand. Similarly, an increase in voter registration might be attributed to the block workers'
efforts and regarded as one of the anticipated results of this type of program.

   As we have stressed throughout this book, however, program formulation is at best a nebulous process. Little is really known of the benefits provided
by many social service programs. For the most part,
we have also made the tacit assumption that the consumer, if he knew the value of these services, would
be willing to pay the costs of producing them. At
best, this is a guess that needs to be validated over
the long term. Except for a few projects with immediately measurable results, the output of most social
service programs can only be measured in the long term
and even then only in the grossest of ways. This is
so because the individuals who are the focus of these
programs are subject to a great many factors other
than those directly involved in the social service
project. At the same time, the inability to measure
anticipated results cannot be used as an excuse for
not predicting what these results are expected to be,
and how they are to be measured. A statement of goals
should set up the requirements of functions to be
performed. This rationalizing process, i.e., the development of congruency between goals and functions,
should be validated by a statement of anticipated results which is logically consistent with the performed
functions. In other words, the entire rationale for
a project should be subjected to a test of consistency
and relevancy as validated by anticipated results.
The fact that the state of the art of the social sciences allows for only approximate measurement of anticipated results should not be used as an excuse for
not attempting the measurement process. However,
measuring anticipated results is not the totality of
the evaluation process.

                     EVALUATION PROCEDURES

   The evaluation procedures with which this section
is concerned are independent of the measurement of

anticipated results discussed earlier. Rather, the
evaluation process is, in this case, concerned with
project design and project implementation.

Returning to our industrial site development
project, the concern of the evaluation process here
should be on such factors as the number of industrial
contacts needed to generate one completed project,
the costs of these contacts, techniques for reducing
these costs without impairing program effectiveness,
and similar factors. An assessment also needs to be
made of the competency of the staff personnel, the
type of background that they need to develop and implement programs of this type, and ways for upgrading
their skills.

Measures of staff efficiency and effectiveness
can also be made by making estimates of the complexity of the problems with which they were involved,
the need for inter-agency cooperation, and so forth,
and how the staff dealt with these issues. Critical
to this evaluation, also, is an awareness of their
ability to tap available reservoirs of knowledge and
skill of personnel normally available to them.

By reviewing these processes, if only in a descriptive manner, program strengths and weaknesses
can be identified and solutions, if available, suggested for these weaknesses. Conversely, every effort
should be made to identify areas where corrections in
procedures cannot be made in order to avoid too strin-
gent a control of staff procedures or a needless criticism of staff procedures.

As in the instance of measuring anticipated results, those functions that will be needed to develop
and implement a project must be defined. These functions must then be related to a series of tasks that
are to be performed by staff personnel individually
or collectively. By providing a provisional flow
chart of tasks to be accomplished, job descriptions
can be written. Shortcomings either in the task
descriptions or staff performance can then be assessed and, from this basic assessment, an evaluation
of overall project efficiency made.

Once again, the process of developing a statement of tasks to be performed is arduous. It is essential, however, if adequate emphasis is to be placed on the evaluation process.

Retrospectively tracing task requirements and task performance can, if properly done, indicate the technical viability of a goals superstructure. Some desirable outputs can be obtained only in theory. The complexities of the real world may not allow for the development of an extremely vital project. For example, many of the industrial firms with whom we had contact during our research phase did not want to enter into a 20-year lease. This was too long a period of time for them to comprehend. In many cases, the managers of these small firms planned to retire before the expiration of the lease and felt that their personal liberty would be circumscribed by the length of the lease. In one sense, this notion is irrational; management should, in theory, provide for its own replacement, and this replacement should be with the firm when the original manager retires. Few of the owners of small businesses, irrespective of their financial success, care to think in these terms. The firm is their private creation. The business co-exists with them. When the time comes to retire, they will either liquidate or sell the firm and, at that point in time, they do not want to be encumbered by a lease. Thus, the ability of the staff personnel may be limited by the perspectives of the people with whom they have to deal. And these perspectives need not be rooted in reality. Program goals and approaches may have to be altered to fit the irrational realities of the situation.

Similarly, the managers of the industrial firms with whom the staff must deal may insist on an extremely high level of staff expertise in business management techniques, if only because of their inherent trust in other business people and their similar mistrust of social welfare types. The structure of the social welfare organization may have to be amended to meet their need for credibility.

In the case of a project staff that must deal simultaneously with target area residents, tenants, and

lending institutions, this may impose on the project
a larger-sized staff than originally anticipated. The
community at large may require one type of person,
and the business community another, such that these
two staff personnel may only interact with one specific group of outsiders. This can cause conflict in
the internal management of the project, thus requiring a project hierarchy capable of dealing with intra-
organizational conflict.

In summary, the entire process of discovering the
need for a project, developing the project itself,
recruiting and training required staff personnel, establishing needed liaison with relevant city agencies,
target area groups, and representatives of the community at large, is a vast and complex undertaking.
At best, the process can be made less painful and
difficult by structuring the procedures that will be
essential to each part of the process, and by developing a relevant administrative mode and mechanism.
Trial and error will be part of the game, as modes of
operations will have to be searched out and tested
against realities. Inevitably, the complexities of
the problem will be understated and the simplicities
overstated. Few of us are capable of comprehending
the complexity of an ongoing organization, irrespective of its size. Even fewer of us are able to explain this complexity in simple, communicative terms.
Because of this, guidelines for program philosophy,
development, and implementation are essential. The
purpose of this book is to provide a description of
this process as it was worked out in New York City,
and to objectify as much of this experience that
others can avoid at least some of the mistakes that
we made in learning to live with the social welfare
planning process.

APPENDIXES

APPENDIX A

CRITERIA TERMS DEFINED

1. <u>Funds</u>

    a. <u>Concentrated</u> (1 point). Refers to the potential of concentrating all Model Cities funds in the Model Cities area. Some funds by regulation or legislative intent cannot be spent wholly in the Model Cities area. The aim of this criterion is to identify programs whose funding can be placed in one area to gain the maximum impact.

    b. <u>Some Concentration</u> (1/2 point). Some agencies, especially city-wide, can utilize some applicants, or place some of their program money into a Model Cities area. If this amounts to 25 per cent to 50 per cent, then it is placed in this category.

    c. <u>Dispersion</u> (0). Those programs whose funds are dispersed so thinly that they hardly affect a Model Cities area are placed in this category. This criterion refers to those programs where less than 25 per cent of the allocated program fund is used in the Model Cities area.

2. <u>Related to Urban Renewal or Vest Pocket Housing</u>

    a. <u>Related to Urban Renewal Program</u> (1 point). If a program can be tied in with some aspect of the urban renewal program, then this tends to support one of the basic intents of the Model Cities legislation: the input of physical and human resources to assist a low-income area. The degree of relationship is not being considered.

    b. <u>Not Related to Urban Renewal Program</u> (0).

3. Initiation of Program

a. 0-12 Months (1 point). Those programs that
can be in operation within a year from the date they
are funded are in keeping with the Model Cities legislation, i.e., to bring new programs into the community as soon as possible.

b. 1 Year and Over (0). This dichotomy of rat-
ings unfortunately gives no consideration to the possibility that a program that requires a longer period
of time to develop may actually produce the best and
most effective results. Because of the point system,
however, this criterion in and of itself does not
rule out the possible acceptance of such programs.

4. Attract Private Resources

a. Yes (1 point). Any program that can attract
additional resources from the private sector should
be given high priority because it permits the public
sector to use its resources for other programs that
the private sector may not normally assist. By resources are meant funds, facilities, and personnel.
The resources may come from any segment of the private sector: a university, business, religious, or
welfare group.

b. No (0 point). Self-explanatory.

5. Desired by Local Citizens

a. Program Well Accepted (1 point). A program
should have popular citizen support. It is possible
that people will strongly support a program that
serves only specific target populations (such as Meals
on Wheels for the house-bound aged), but may reject a
broad-gauged program (such as slum clearance). Thus,
this criterion refers to how favorably a cross-section
of the Model Cities population views a proposed program.

b. Mixed Acceptance (1/2 point). Some programs
may receive a mixed reception from the citizens. A
narcotics center or a halfway house for paroled ex-
convicts are examples of this type of program.

c. Little Acceptance (0 point). Programs that
the citizens have either rejected or are indifferent
to, irrespective of whether the professional planner
considers them valuable or not.

6. Emphasis on Rehabilitation and Prevention

a. Rehabilitation and Prevention Concurrently
(1 point). Rehabilitation assumes that a program
will repair some damage that has already been done
to the behavior, attitudes, or skills of a person
and/or the environmental situation in which he lives
(housing, streets, sanitation). Prevention assumes
that a program aims at the maintenance or development
of a person or his surrounding environment consistent
with the standards or norms of the general society.

Given these assumptions, any program that
combines both of these aspects in it is given the
full point score.

b. Rehabilitation Only or Prevention Only (1/2
point). A program that has only one of these features
is considered slightly less valuable than one that
has both. A Head Start program that uses only professional teachers is categorized as prevention only.
If it employs neighborhood mothers and places them on
a career ladder then it combines both segments. Most
skill training programs are only rehabilitative, however.

7. Utilization of Local Citizens

a. To a Considerable Degree (1 point). Utilization of local citizens refers to whether the program
employs them as staff or requires them to set policy.
It does not refer to them as consumers of the programs
and services such as a person who is being trained
for a position. If at least 50 per cent of the persons who operate the program (whether paid or volunteer) are from the Model Cities area, the program is
given a high rating.

b. Some Utilization (1/2 point). Local persons
are involved in operating the program in less than
50 per cent of the positions.

c. Not Utilized (0 point). Self-explanatory.

8. Related to Other Programs

a. Related to Two or More Other Programs (1
point). A program that is mounted in the Model Cities area that requires the cooperation and coordination of two or more other existing programs to be
effective is given the first point because of the
emphasis on coordination of existing programs called
for in the Model Cities legislation. Thus, a manpower program that requires the assistance of the
unions to implement a program would be given one full
point.

b. Related to One Program (1/2 point). Self-
explanatory.

c. Stands Alone (0). Self-explanatory.

The basis for selecting these criteria is their
relevance to the Model Cities legislation. Because
there is no objective way of weighing a criterion,
all criteria have been given equal weight. However,
it should be noted that this weighing system is retro
spective; it does not attempt to predict the effectiveness of a program once it has been brought into
operation.

APPENDIX B

RANKINGS OF HRA PROGRAMS

In order to test the criteria for ranking programs that were discussed in Chapter 3, a number of ongoing HRA programs were reviewed and ranked. The following pages show how the ranking points were distributed for each program. The criteria that were used were admittedly crude because we wanted nonprofessionals to be able to use these criteria and thus be able to participate in the planning process. Similarly, the programs that we suggested are crude and admittedly unsophisticated. However, the outcome of both of these processes can be extremely sophisticated and this is what we wanted. The function of the Model Cities process is to help people, and not a sophisticated planning or administrative process.

TABLE 2

Setting of Priority of Social Programs

(Illustrative Sample)

PROGRAM CRITERIA

Name of Program by Agency	A Funds: Model Cities Area Only (1)	A Funds: Some in Model Cities (1/2)	A Funds: Little in Model Cities (0)	B Urban Renewal Related: Yes (1)	B: No (0)	C Quickly Mounted: 0-12 (1)	C: 12-over (0)	D Attract Private Resources: Yes (1)	D: No (0)	E Desired by People: Yes (1)	E: Some (1/2)	E: No (0)	F Emphasis on Rehab. & Prev.: Prev. (1)	F: Rehab. (1/2)	F: Mainly Prev. (0)	G Utilize Local Citizens: Yes (1)	G: Some (1/2)	G: No (0)	H Related to Other Programs: (1) (2-1/2)	H: (1/2) (1)	H: (0)	Total Points
1. Concentrated Employment	X				X	X		X		X			X			X			X			6.5
2. Neighborhood Youth Corps		X			X	X			X					X		X				X		4
3. Police Athletic League		X			X	X			X					X			X				X	3

CDA	A Funds Concentrated	A Funds Both	A Funds Dispersed	B Related to HDA Yes	B Related to HDA No	C Quickly Mounted 0-12	C Quickly Mounted 12-over	D Attract Private Resources Yes	D Attract Private Resources No	E Desired by People Yes	E Desired by People No	F Prev. & Rehab.	F Rehab.	F Prev.	G Utilize Local Citizens Yes	G Utilize Local Citizens No	H 2-1/2	H 1	H 0	Total Points
4. Early Childhood	X				X	X			X	X		X			X		X			6
5. Family Planning	X				X	X			X	?				X	X		X			4.5
6. Multi-Service Centers		X		X			X	X		X		X			X		X			7
7. Health Centers	X				X		X	X		X		X			X		X			6
8. Mobile Medical Dental Units for Homebound	X				X	X		X		X		X			X		X			7
9. Cooperative Housing	X			X		X		X		X			X		X		X			7.5
10. Center of Innovation (pre-K to 2nd gr.)	X				X	X		X		X				X	X		X			6
11. Career Ladder Concepts	X				X	X			X	X		X			X		X			6
12. Vocational Ed. in school after school hours	X				X	X		X		X				X	X		X			6.5
13. Legal services for poor		X			X	X			X	X				X	X		X			6

(continued)

TABLE 2 (Continued)

PROGRAM CRITERIA

Program Misc.	A Funds			B Related to HDA		C Quickly Mounted		D Attract Private Resources		E Desired by People		F Emphasis on Rehab. & Prev.			G Utilize Local Citizens		H Related to Other Programs			Total Points
	Concentrated	Dispersed	Both	Yes	No	0-12	12-over	Yes	No	Yes	No	Rehab. & Prev.	Rehab.	Prev.	Yes	No	2 1/2	1	0	
14. No Bail Project			X		X	X			X	X				X		X			X	3
15. 24-Hour Court			X		X	X			X	X				X		X			X	3
16. Mini-bussing (work-business)	X			X		X		X		X		X			X		X			8
17. Residential Youth Center	X			X		X		X		?			X		X		X			6.5
18. Older adults supervise Youth in Recreation Program	X				X	X			X	X		X			X		X			6
19. Housing office rentals	X			X		X		X		X		X			X		X			8
20. Newcomer Adjustment	X			X		X			X	X			X		X		X			6.5
21. Small business assistance office (tech.-finan. asst.)	X				X	X		X			?		X			X	X			4.5
22. Emergency temporary housing	X			X			X	X			?			X		X	X			4.5
23. Housing workshop clinics (tenant-landlord rel. to maintain homes)	X			X		X		X			?			X	X		X			6.5
24. Industry--operate schools (test teaching devices on children)	X			X		X		X		X				X	X		X			6.5

PROGRAM CRITERIA

Name of Program by Agency	Funds Concen-trated (1)	(1/2)	Dis-persed (0)	Related to HDA Yes (1)	No (0)	Quickly Mounted 0-12 (1)	12-over (0)	Attract Private Resources Yes (1)	No (0)	Desired by People Yes (1)	(1/2)	No (0)	Emphasis on Rehab. & Prev. (1)	Rehab. Mainly (1/2)	Prev. Mainly (0)	Utilize Local Citizens Yes (1)	(1/2)	No (0)	Related to Other Programs (21) (1)	7 (1/2)	0 (2)	Total Points
MCDA																						
A. Skill Training																						6
25. Scheuer		X			X	X		X						X		X			X			
26. Job Counseling (Board of Education)		X			X	X			X				X					X		X		3

(Continued)

TABLE 2 (Continued)

PROGRAM CRITERIA

Misc.	Funds Concen-trated	Funds Both	Funds Dis-persed	Related to HDA Yes	Related to HDA No	Quickly Mounted 0-12	Quickly Mounted 12-over	Attract Private Resources Yes	Attract Private Resources No	Desired by People Yes	Desired by People Sme	Desired by People No	Emphasis Rehab. & Prev.	Emphasis Rehab.	Emphasis Prev.	Uses Local Citizens Yes	Uses Local Citizens No	Related to Other Programs 2 1/2	Related to Other Programs 1	Related to Other Programs 0	Total Points
27. Street Workers	X				X	X			X	X			X			X			X		6
28. Welfare Center	X				X		X		X	X				X		X			X		4.5
29. Central Data Bank	X			X			X		X			X			X		X		X		3.5
30. Community College (2 years)	X			X			X	X		X					X	X			X		6.5
31. Street Academies	X				X	X		X				X		X		X			X		6

APPENDIX C

WORK PROGRAMS: PROPOSALS TO THE
MAYOR'S MODEL CITIES COMMITTEE

In late 1967, the progress of the Model Cities
Planning Group was reviewed and assessed. A statement of the work program proposed for this planning
group was requested at that time. In addition, the
Model Cities planning group and the planning groups
then in existence in the Manpower Career and Development Agency, the Community Development Agency, and
the Department of Social Services were asked to prepare programs for incorporation in the Model Cities
program. The following proposals were received for
review by the Mayor's Model Cities Committee.

I.   OPPORTUNITY CENTERS

As stated in the program outline for the Opportunity Centers, MCDA has requested approximately $39 million in capital funds for the construction of eleven Opportunity Centers in eleven regions of the city covering all five boroughs. At a minimum, three and possibly five Opportunity Centers will be located in those areas designated as Model Cities areas. MCDA strongly feels that the Opportunity Centers, a permanent system for the delivery of comprehensive manpower services to the disadvantaged areas of New York City, is a vital and necessary input into the Model Cities program.

The Opportunity Centers and the Neighborhood Manpower Service Centers which support the Opportunity Center's outreach and recruitment functions, constitute the largest-scale attempt of the various city, state, and federal agencies in New York City to offer their services in one coordinated effort; e.g., since the inception of the Opportunity Centers concept, the Department of Social Services has agreed to use the Opportunity Centers as the regional office for its Division of Employment and Rehabilitation, thus, in fact, tying together the services of the Department of Social Services and the Manpower and Career Development Agency.

The participation of other agencies and groups in the OC program was clearly stated in the program outline.

In the initial planning stages of the OC system, the New York City Council Against Poverty was involved. In addition, MCDA works directly with the community corporations in each of the poverty areas of the city, through contractual agreements for the operation of Neighborhood Manpower Centers, the foundation of a basic manpower system for New York City. MCDA has included, within the general plan, plans for the creation of a lay advisory board for the Opportunity Centers.

MCDA will move to set up the OC system in each of the Model Cities areas within the next fiscal year.

The various components of the program will be temporarily housed in existing facilities until such time
as the construction of the Ocs is completed. Although
MCDA has requested capital funds for construction,
additional federal monies will be needed to lease and
rehabilitate existing facilities to meet the demands
of a program and system which will be able to provide
extensive training and supportive services for above
2,000 persons per annum, per center.

To a large extent, training in the Opportunities
Centers will relate directly to planned and ongoing
activities in the Model Cities areas. The centers
will be equipped to train residents of the Model
Cities areas for the various jobs created in construction, etc., by that program.

MCDA estimates rent and rehabilitation costs at
$2.13 million per annum for five centers, all of which
will be in the Model Cities areas. This estimate is
based on total space requirements for all five centers
of 534,162 square feet. The multiplier is a cost of
$4.00 per square foot for rent and rehabilitation.

II. NEIGHBORHOOD SERVICE CENTERS

A multi-service center is a means to bring about
a coordination of all city, private, and community
operated services in a defined geographical area. In
addition to being the visual and functional nerve
center of a neighborhood service program, the facility will house a wide range of actual decentralized
services, the mix depending upon community and agency
priorities, resources, and the existing service facilities already functioning in the target area. The
centers now in planning will contain approximately
40,000 square feet of space and cost between $1.5
and $2 million apiece. Their effective service areas
will be smaller than most of the city's poverty areas,
serving a neighborhood of about 50,000 people.

Centers are projected for Model Cities areas.
Presently, five new multi-service facilities are under consideration, to be funded during the coming

year under section 703 of the HUD Act. Their locations will be: Hunts Point and Brownsville.

The Hunts Point multi-service center is the core
service facility of New York's Pilot NSP area. HUD
funds are presently reserved for this building. An
application has been submitted for the Brownsville
center; planning for East Harlem is now underway. In
all of these areas, the HDA has worked closely with
community planning bodies organized through the assistance of CDA by the local community corporations.
In Hunts Point, due to the nature of the Pilot NSP
program, community participation in the planning has
been especially strong. Through an OEO Demonstration
grant, a community staff of fifteen, plus consultants,
is working with fourteen neighborhood committees and
the parent multi-service board to develop program and
facility plans. HDA has engaged a team of consultants
to act as its delegate in Hunts Point. Working in the
same field office with the local staff, this team is
responsible for coordinating the total planning effort, and also for developing models and prototypes
that will be useful in designing the subsequent facilities.

The preliminary facility plan for Hunts Point will
be completed by the end of March, 1968. Detailed
architectural planning will take four to six months
longer. With the Hunts Point prototype fully developed by June, 1968, the planning period for Brownsville and other centers should be considerably
shortened. The relationship between program and facility planning in each case being unique, exact
planning periods cannot be specified at this time.

In the Hunts Point program, well over $250,000
will go into total planning for facility and program.
In the other areas at least half this amount could
well be required for agency planning input and community advocate planning assistance.

Each center will require some $600,000 in city
funds and $1,000,000 in federal funds for construc-
tion, in addition to the $125,000 required for program
and facility planning.

Nearly every city agency and private agency, hospital, college, etc., rendering service to the community has an actual or potential role in the neighborhood service programs and multi-service centers. Those directly involved in Hunts Point to date are indicated in the following summary.

III. FAMILY DAY CARE

Family Day Care is a program that has three objectives.

The first is a method to take care of children of AFDC mothers to permit these mothers to undertake job training and/or full-time jobs.

Second, it is aimed at providing training for another set of AFDC mothers in the care of small children. This training of the Family Day Care mothers may later qualify them for career opportunities in day care centers, Head Start, pre-kindergarten, or other work with children.

This program was planned by HRA staff, the Board of Education, the Health Service Administration, and the Council Against Poverty. Funds from OEO, Head Start program were initially used to implement the program, now in existence in the Model Cities area. In the coming year it is expected that the twenty Family Day Care programs will be started. The Model Cities Citizens Council, when formed, will play an integral part in the planning of these additional centers.

IV. ECONOMIC DEVELOPMENT PROGRAM

Following are the programs in economic development proposed for the Model Cities application and information as to their structure.

(1) Establishment of Local Development Corporations and Small Business Investment Corporations to service each Model Cities area.

The work tasks involved will include encouraging the community, business, and banking interests to invest in these Conduit Corporations; encouraging banks to make loans to individuals who want to invest in these corporations; and to get the loss structured so that they can be the vehicle for federal loan monies coming into the Model Cities areas. The work task also involves integrating the reorganized services of existing Small Business Development Opportunity Centers with these Conduit Corporations.

The time period for establishing these Corporations is one year.

The planning cost of establishing these economic tools is estimated at $500,000. The anticipated sources of funds are a combination of a Model Cities grant, Labor Department grant, Economic Development Agency funds and tax levied moneies. The funds for continuing and reorganizing of the Small Business Development Opportunity Centers will come from the Office of Economic Opportunity, administered through the Small Business Administration.

(2) Organizing minority-group general contractors, subcontractors, and architects in the construction industry through their trade association so that they can fully participate in renovating, construction, and demolition contracts in the Model Cities area.

The work task involves aiding in the restructuring of the trade associations so that they will be able to assume responsibilities for training the membership in bidding, and fiscal management practice. In addition, we would help them to assume responsibilities for on-the-job training programs with this program funded by the Manpower and Career Development Agency.

Finally, we will help them work out the
problems of securing bid and performance
bonds.

The time period for this process is two
years. The planning cost for this program
is expected to be about $100,000 over two
years and the potential source of funds are
Ford Foundation, Model Cities grant, and
tax-levied monies.

The planning staff will be members of
the staff of HRA with experience in the
area of economics, insurance, and construction trades.

(3) Organizing minority real-estate boards so
that they will be able to take advantage
of new opportunities to manage city property in Model Cities areas between the time
of condemnation and demolition; planning
the new opportunities for greater participation by minority groups in city contracts.
Utilization of our Manpower Training Centers
as outposts for training programs on the
managing of city property is anticipated.

Time period: one year.

The planning costs are $75,000. Source
of funds: Model Cities grant and the Manpower and Career Development Agency. Responsible planning staff will be individuals
who have background in the real-estate field
and general economic development.

General Statement

There is a distinction between fundamental planning and that part of planning which also is in fact
implementation. In the case of these programs, the
implementation is another dimension of planning because these new institutional structures must be developed before they can begin to function in a
meaningful, implementative way. For example, the

Local Development Corporations and the Small Business
Investment Corporations are operational when the flow
of federal money comes through. Therefore, the
setting-up of such corporations is in fact an aspect
of planning.

V.   DEPARTMENT OF SOCIAL SERVICES--PLANNING
FOR MODEL CITIES

The New York City Department of Social Services,
in its effort to expand, decentralize, and reintegrate
its services responsively at the community level, is
committed to the Model Cities concept, a concept which
requires not merely the decentralization of traditional service outputs, but a concentration of increased
agency--and inter-agency--planning and material resources in Model Cities areas. Operating as given
throughout the planning and service delivery process
is the commitment to maximize both inter-agency linkages and the participation of the community. The
department welcomes the opportunity to consider these
three Model Cities areas as the locus for program innovation and development. Briefly, these are some
of the "milestones" in the agency's movement within
Model Cities to become, in fact as well as in name,
the Department of Social Services:

(1) In the urban renewal areas within Model
    Cities boundaries, the department is com-
    mited, within the 1968-69 fiscal year, to
    the staffing of neighborhood service cen-
    ters and participation through these centers
    in an inter-agency multi-service system.

(2) In the Hunts Point pilot project within the
    South Bronx Model Cities area, the depart-
    ment will staff two neighborhood service
    centers and explore with the community al-
    ternatives for maximizing its participation
    in essential decision making as mandated by
    the community's OEO-207 grant.

(3) The department is moving toward redefining
    its role as the social utility for the entire

community regardless of the need for public
assistance. Perhaps nowhere is the need
for services to the non-public assistance
population so evident as in situations requiring physical relocation of individuals
and families. In close cooperation with
the New York City Housing Authority and the
Department of Relocation, the Department of
Social Services will shortly be staffing
seven units to provide a full range of social
services in the relocation process for vest-
pocket housing sites.

(4) Working closely with planning staff of the
Human Resources Administration and professional and para-professional staff of local
Head Start delegate agencies, the department
is currently participating in New York City's
Family Day Care program, an innovative response to the child care and work experience
needs of poverty group mothers. The department is currently outstationing Bureau of
Child Welfare staff in the ten Head Start
Family Day Care centers. It is hoped that
the experience with these pilot centers will
validate the expansion of the program throughout the Model Cities areas.

(5) It has become increasingly evident that in
order for a service delivery system to respond appropriately to the varying needs of
people, it must contain a variety of levels
of expertise and knowledge of the community--
from the "neighborhood wisdom" of the case
aide to the clinical skill of a professionally trained social worker. The department
has laid the groundwork for movement in this
direction by the introduction of 450 case
aide trainees under the Scheuer program and
the appointment of approximately 450 senior
case workers. We have asked the New York
City Department of Personnel and the State
Department of Social Services for authoriza-
tion to establish the civil service positions
of case aide and assistant case worker, thus

guaranteeing both a career ladder for the
non-professional and the manpower essential
for the forthcoming pilot project on the
differential utilization of staff--the team
concept in the delivery of public social
service. Several varying models for demonstration purposes have been identified and
it is expected that these models will be
utilized on a pilot basis during 1968 in the
service delivery systems in Model Cities
areas.

(6) Discussion of planning for the expansion of
social services should not obscure the fact
that one of the major missions of this agency is to maximize the income maintenance
function--to provide a minimum standard of
living with maximum dignity to the community
in need. Central to this notion is the sep-
aration of the income maintenance and social
service functions, a project currently in the
planning stages, but expected to be given
highest priority in the coming year. It is
hoped that a pilot project can be implemented
during the first half of the 1968-69 fiscal
year.

The commitment to program development must be
matched, if that commitment is to become a reality,
by a commitment to adequate staffing. If the department's variety of program designs for and with the
Model Cities communities are to be maximized, and if
the areas are to be considered as far as possible
as unities, a number of programmatic staffing requirements become paramount.

(1) There should be a director of social services for each of the Model Cities areas
who, with staff assistance, is responsible
for coordinating and directing the various
departmental "inputs."

(2) Experience in the development and implementation of new programs has made it clear
that there must be a built-in training

component--a numerically adequate training staff to design and in some cases implement a training program for all involved staff, including inter-agency groups of staff.

(3) The department has made a commitment which is essential if the planning process is to be rationalized--that every new program or complex of programs, whether intra- or inter-agency, have a built-in evaluation component. We see the need for increased research staff to meet that commitment.

(4) Planning for an implementation of Model Cities efforts is also a community organization process, if the community is in fact to be meaningfully involved in the planning and delivery of services. It will take a combination of professional and para-professional community organization skill to stimulate and support this process. Hopefully, partial financial support for this process will be available from Model Cities planning funds.

VI.   SOCIAL SERVICES IN VEST-POCKET HOUSING

In the first round of vest-pocket housing, the Housing Authority has made space available for community facilities, either in separate community buildings or in the housing units themselves. HDA has been planning with HRA, the housing citizen councils, and the community corporations for the best use of this space for social and recreational programs. Meetings have taken place on a continuous basis to discuss the introduction of such services as a children's center, a community center, a center for the aged, group day care centers, tenant meeting space, a complete recreational and cultural center, and facilities to provide outreach services from the proposed or operating multi-service centers. Under consideration are such services as addiction programs, legal services, manpower counseling, welfare services, and health services.

The planning for such services is currently under discussion by the interested groups noted above. It is expected that the planning will be completed by January or February in the East New York and Bedford-Stuyvesant vest-pocket areas but will take longer in the Mott Haven and Milbank-Frawley (Harlem) areas. Planning costs are being paid out of city tax levy funds and the use of existing staff.

In round two of vest-pocket housing, the experience gained in this past year will result in a wider range of social and cultural activities being placed in these areas as well as a closer integration between physical and social planning. Model Cities supplemental funds will be required to implement some of these services.

VII. YOUTH ACTIVITIES

HRA is planning to direct a service to reach individual youth twelve to twenty-one years of age, in each of the three Model Cities areas as an outreach program directed to the disoriented and alienated youth, boys and girls. These services will be operated by the Youth Service Agency in the multiservice centers.

The Community Corporations, the Board of Education, and the Manpower and Career Development Agency will share in the planning and implementation of these services. The extension of these new concentrated services in the Hunts Point NSP is currently being negotiated with the NSP citizen committee in that area. Model Cities funds will be required to implement the program. Existing planning staffs in the several agencies are all that is required to work out the plans for these services. When it is feasible, youth activities will also be placed in the vest-pocket housing community facilities.

VIII. EDUCATIONAL PROGRAMS

Below are listed some of the programs which we are thinking about for the educational component of

Model Cities. They are still in the formative stage
and we can only give limited information at this time.

(1) A homework helpers program whereby seniors
    and juniors of high schools will be hired
    to tutor elementary school children.

(2) Adult education classes to teach the parents
    the current methods taught in the schools so
    that they can help their children (i.e., new
    math).

(3) Family assistants to aid the family in help-
    ing their children.

(4) A program of assisting the children who drop
    out through encouraging them to return to
    school, to join vocational training programs,
    etc.

(5) A program whereby children in pre-school
    programs will come under the aegis of a per-
    son who would be trained to arrange educa-
    tional supports and to be responsible for the
    child throughout his school career. The
    person would also work with parents and pa-
    rent groups at the block and neighborhood
    level.

(6) An increase in Head Start and pre-kindergarten
    programs will be recommended as well as an
    emphasis on a program of "follow-through" in-
    to the early childhood education years.
    These programs should be better coordinated
    among the different agencies and will include
    complete service from pre-natal care to
    second-grade curriculum.

(7) A central service area where people can be
    directed toward different kinds of education
    and training programs which might be tied up
    with such other service directives as health,
    housing, sanitation.

(8) Student service centers: High school stu-
    dents will run the centers and evaluate

community needs and determine how the high
school can be used to meet these needs. Pos-
sibly involving curriculum experimentation.

Various kinds of physical structures will be
necessary to house these programs, as well as a variety of hard and software equipment. Apart from
rooms in the vest-pocket housing which, hopefully,
will be used for persons living in the immediate
neighborhoods as well as in the housing itself, multi-
service centers, and combination day care, Head Start,
and after-school study centers will be needed.

The service area for these programs will include
the entire Model Cities neighborhood as designated.

IX. HEALTH CENTER PROGRAM

I. Name and Purpose

The 211-2 Neighborhood Center Program is designed
to provide comprehensive family-centered medical care
for 80 per cent of the medical needs of a population
of 30,000 through a neighborhood-based facility. The
service design will be a number of medical care teams
consisting of a physician, nurse, public health nurse,
social worker, and several neighborhood health workers responsible for and feasible to the needs of individual family units.

II. Relationship to Community Corporation

The community corporation is the appropriate
reviewing body for 211 programs. Each neighborhood
health council has representatives on the Community
Corporation's Health Committee, and the Community
Corporation. The Health Committee of the Community
Corporation, in turn, has at least two members on
the Health Council.

III. Facilities Located in Model Cities Areas

      (a) Agency and site
      (b) Funding source
      (c) Planning and/or implementation stages
      (d) Citizen roles

1. St. John's Provident

    (a) Bedford-Stuyvesant; within triangle of
Stuyvesant, Broadway, and Atlantic. Exact location to be determined.

    (b) Provident Clinical Society of Brooklyn
was granted $1,679,294 to initiate com-
prehensive medical services.

    (c) Grant period July 1, 1967-June 30, 1968.

    (d) Health Committee of YIA (Youth In Action)
has been doing general program and site
selection. Once site is finally selected, a health council composed of persons
from service area will be formed.

2. Hunts Point

    (a) The Department of Health has requested
a site bounded by 152nd Street, Union
Avenue, 151st Street and Prospect Avenue.

    (b) Construction costs to come out of capital
budget funds. Operating costs to be supported by Title IX monies. Planning
monies will be requested under section
314E of Public Health Service Act:
$260,000.

    (c) The Health Subcommittee and outside staff
assistance of the Neighborhood Service
Program propose a one-year planning and
exploratory phase to determine practica-
bility of group practice as a functional
medical delivery system.

    (d) Hunts Point Community Corporation Health
Subcommittee has over-all governing responsibility.

3. Morrisania

    (a) Lincoln Hospital, the Bronx Lebanon Hos-
pital Center and the Morrisania Community

have been developing a 211-2 proposal for
health areas 21.20, 28 or 29 for 1968 sub-
mission.

X.   MATERNAL EDUCATION

(1) This project will help provide a stimulating
environment for children under three years
by demonstrating behavior to the mother which
encourages and stimulates the child's development. At the same time it will provide
employment to women who live in the community
who will teach parents those child care techniques which will reinforce the development
of the child. This job will be part of a
career ladder that may lead to a professional
degree of social work or nursing.

(2) The Health Department will include this program in its Health Guide proposal which is
funded by a grant from the state. The Health
Guides will also become part of the Public
Service Career Program (Scheuer). Funding
will therefore be shared by MCDA.

XI.   COMMUNITY ACTION FOR LEGAL SERVICES, INC.

Community Action for Legal Services, Inc. (CALS)
renders services as the city-wide coordinating agency
for the provision of legal services in New York City.
CALS will receive all funds from the Office of Economic Opportunity for legal services and will contract
with ten local corporations for the operation of
neighborhood law offices. Four of the corporations
are:

> Legal Aid Society
> Mobilization for Youth Legal Services Unit
> Bedford-Stuyvesant Legal Services Corporation
> Harlem Assertion of Rights, Inc. (HAR)

The remaining six corporations are to be established to provide services in various neighborhoods.

The Legal Aid Society and Mobilization for Youth are
presently in effective existence.

The following programs will operate in Model
Cities areas: In New York County, Manhattan Legal
Services Corporation A will operate offices in East
Harlem, and Harlem Association of Rights, Inc. (HAR),
will operate offices in Central Harlem and the Upper
West Side.

In Bronx County, Bronx Legal Services Corporation
A will have offices in South Bronx and Morrisania,
and Bronx Legal Services Corporation B will have an
office or offices in Hunts Point. In Kings County,
Brooklyn Legal Services Corporation A will operate
offices in Brownsville and East New York, and Bedford-
Stuyvesant Legal Services Corporation will have offices in the Bedford-Stuyvesant area.

Except for completing the formation of boards of
directors of local operating corporations, Community
Action for Legal Services, Inc., has substantially
completed the planning stage for the time being and
has now undertaken its implementation stage. Agencies involved in the planning of the program included
the Council Against Poverty, the legal staff of Community Development Agency, the Association of the Bar
of the City of New York, the New York County Lawyers
Association, several county bar associations, and
various representatives of the poor community.

XII. FAMILY PLANNING PROGRAMS IN
MODEL CITIES AREAS

These are simple-to-mount programs meeting health
and social needs--desirable services from the patient's point of view which should be accessible and
available and can easily utilize space exclusively or
shared with another health service during "down" times.
Existing services in institutions such as hospitals,
health centers, and child health stations can be expanded or new facilities can be provided.

Agencies currently involved in providing service
include:

(1) Municipal and voluntary hospitals, especially those with active obstetrical services;

(2) Maternal and infant care programs located
in certain Health Department facilities,
utilizing money from the Children's Bureau,
Department of Health, Education, and Welfare;

(3) Planned Parenthood of New York City which
operates free-standing, single-purpose
services funded through its non-profit
status;

(4) Some private physicians, primarily OB-GYN
specialists, although some general practitioners also provide contraceptive supplies;

(5) OEO comprehensive medical care centers (in
Bedford-Stuyvesant).

Potential Sources of Funding:

(1) Medicaid (via voluntary hospitals/private
physicians)

(2) Municipal budget for Departments of Health
and Hospitals

(3) Federal funds via Children's Bureau; large
and increasing amounts earmarked for family
planning for next five years beginning July,
1968

(4) OEO-Sec. 205,211 funds; some from HRA tax-
levy funds

(5) Social Security welfare amendments

Timetable for Planning and Implementation:

(1) Up to six months for planning

(2) Additional six months to eighteen months for
implementation, depending upon physical
facilities available

Staff Needs:

Existing planning staff of involved agencies
consists of about five or six persons, only two
of whom are working full time.

Additional staff needs are for six full-time
persons (demographer, planner, and technical
resource persons such as nurses, health educators, program developers).

ABOUT THE AUTHORS

EDWARD M. KAITZ was, until recently, a consultant to the Human Resources Administration of the City of New York, involved in the area of model cities planning and economic development. He worked in conjunction with the Economic Development Administration of the City of New York, the Public Development Corporation, and the City Planning Commission. Through 1969 he was an advisor on economic development to the Public Development Corporation of the City of New York.

Dr. Kaitz was formerly a Senior Staff Associate of Arthur D. Little, Inc., has acted as consultant to the Department of Health, Education and Welfare, and various other federal and state agencies, and has also been a consultant to a number of large-scale corporations. He is currently involved in independent research and consultation in the urban studies area.

Dr. Kaitz received his doctorate in business administration from Harvard University.

HERBERT HARVEY HYMAN is Assistant Professor of Urban Planning at the Department of Urban Affairs, Hunter College, the City University of New York. Previously Dr. Hyman was with New York City's Human Resources Administration (HRA), where as Director of Model Cities Planning he was in charge of planning the major human resources inputs for the City's Model Cities Program. He was also responsible for coordinating the resources in HRA--the largest social welfare agency in the world--with those of other City programs operating in model neighborhoods. Dr. Hyman received his doctorate in social planning from Brandeis University.